CONTENTS

Front Cover—Bog Cotton. (Caitríona Douglas)

Back Cover—A winter view of Atlantic Blanket bog in County Mayo. (Peter Foss)

The IPCC Guide to Irish Peatlands

Edited by

Catherine O'Connell

IRISH PEATLAND
CONSERVATION COUNCIL

CONTRIBUTORS

Dr Richard Bradshaw, School of Botany, Trinity College, Dublin 2.

Dr Seamas Caulfield, Department of Archaeology, University College, Belfield, Dublin 4.

Dr Alan Craig, National Parks & Monuments Service, Office of Public Works, 51 St. Stephens Green, Dublin 2.

Dr John Cross, Research Branch, Wildlife Service, 2 Sidmonton Place, Bray, Co. Wicklow.

Mr David Dunlop, Ulster Trust for Nature Conservation, Barnetts' Cottage, Barnett Demense, Malone Road, Belfast BT9 5PB.

Dr Peter Foss, IPCC, 195 Pearse Street, Dublin 2.

Mr Neil Lockhart, Botany Department, University College Galway, Galway.

Dr Ann Lynch, National Monuments Section, Office of Public Works, 51 St. Stephens Green, Dublin 2.

Mr Brian Madden, IPCC, 195 Pearse Street, Dublin 2.

Ms Catherine O'Connell, IPCC, 195 Pearse Street, Dublin 2.

Dr Barry Raftery, Department of Archaeology, University College, Belfield, Dublin 4.

Dr Martin Speight, Research Branch, Wildlife Service, 2 Sidmonton Place, Bray, Co. Wicklow.

Dr Mary Tubridy, IPCC, 195 Pearse Street, Dublin 2.

Mr Michael Viney, Thallabawn, Westport, Co. Mayo.

Mr Edwin Wymer, 2 Knocklyon Drive, Templeogue, Dublin 14.

ACKNOWLEDGEMENTS

The editor wishes to acknowledge the assistance of the following individuals and organisations for their invaluable help in the production of this book: Michael Casey, Sue Christie, Andy Cole, Tom Curtis, Éamon de Buitléar, Gerry Doyle, Ted Farrell, Peter Foss, Bob Hammond, Oscar Merne, Frank Mitchell, Brian Nolan, David Norris, Jim O'Connor, PJ O'Hare, Tommy O'Shaughnessy, Jim Ryan, John Scarry, Owen Smith, Bob Strickland, James White and John Wilson;

Office of Public Works, Forest & Wildlife Service and An Foras Talúntais.

Special thanks to the artists, Colman Ó'Críodáin and Edwin Wymer, Pauline Bewick and an anonymous collector for allowing us to reproduce "Greater Butterwort on the Bog", Michael Viney for allowing us to reproduce "Under Mweelrea" and the Allied Irish Banks Art Collection for permission to reproduce "West of Ireland Landscape" by James Humbert Craig.

We acknowledge the permission of Faber & Faber Ltd., to reproduce the poem "Bogland" by Seamus Heaney, from *Door Into The Dark*.

The Irish Peatland Conservation Council wishes to acknowledge the generous financial support given by:

Allied Irish Banks plc, Aughinish Alumina Limited, The British Ecological Society, British Petroleum plc, Carrigdhoun Pottery Co-Op Society Limited, Mr A. Cole, An Foras Talúntais, Professor F. Convery, Resource and Environmental Policy Centre, Department of Botany, University College Galway, Electricity Supply Board, Irish Ramblers Club, John Hinde Limited, New Ireland Assurance, Office of Public Works and the Wildlife Service.

The IPCC wishes to acknowledge the financial assistance of the European Community as part of European Year of the Environment 1987.

The opinions expressed by the authors in this book are not necessarily those of the editor or the IPCC.

Cataloging and Publication Data ISBN 0 9512709 0 7

Printed by Fodhla Printing Company Ltd., Dublin.

Irish Peatland Conservation Council, Head Office, 195 Pearse Street, Dublin 2, Ireland.

PREFACE

The Irish Peatland Conservation Council (IPCC), formerly the National Peatland Conservation Committee (NPCC), was founded in 1982 in response to the wholesale destruction of Irish peatlands, the last of their kind in Europe. The IPCC is a non-governmental organisation working to ensure that a representative sample of Irish peatlands are conserved for future generations. We are achieving this through lobbying, publicity, site purchase and education programmes. Our campaign is endorsed by many eminent European scientists and organisations including the World Wildlife Fund and the Dutch Foundation for the Conservation of Irish Bogs.

This book provides a broad range of information on our unique peatland heritage, including the formation of peatlands, their flora and fauna, the history of the use of peatlands and the problems of exploitation and adequate legal protection. The chapters in the book are written by experts chosen because of their practical experience and knowledge of peatlands. The importance of this book is that it is a practical guide designed to encourage people young and old to go out and explore peatlands, whether it is by observing their nature and functioning or simply enjoying the inspirational and aesthetic value of a landscape blanketed by peat.

The chapters on places to visit should help you choose a suitable site to visit. Once you get there the lists of species provided should help you to identify the plant and animal communities typical of peatlands. Further reading and contact addresses are provided for those who wish to delve further into the mysteries of peatlands.

In addition, the information presented should highlight the potential value of peatlands as a teaching tool and we hope that teachers will respond to this. The profits from the sale of this book will be channelled into the "Save the Bogs Campaign" which was launched by the IPCC to purchase threatened peatlands and conserve them for future generations to enjoy.

Catherine O'Connell
Education Officer, IPCC

THE INSPIRATION OF PEATLANDS

Michael Viney

Where I live, on a hillside above the Atlantic, bogland is wrapped around the highest mountain in Connacht like a great brown rug around the knees of an old man—Mweelrea, the bald king, hunched in bony stone above the sea. If you look closer into the rug, you find it woven of rich fabrics—velvety mosses of black and bottle-green, brocaded lichens in gold and rose, filigree trimmings of grey-green lace (Figure 1).

This poetic way of seeing things would mean little to many people. Bogland to them is a bleak wilderness, a brown monotony. Even country people who know the bog well may find nothing especially pleasing or beautiful about it. At best, they think, it is useful, providing fuel and feeding sheep, but almost anything built on it, or planted on it, would probably be an improvement.

The idea of wild landscape of any kind being valuable for itself, or especially beautiful, or an inspiration to poets and writers and artists, is a comparatively modern one. It still feels more natural to some kinds of people than others. If we are to understand the strong feelings that many people have about conserving the bogs—either for or against—and to weigh up what is sometimes called the "inspirational" value of peatland, we need to appreciate the profound changes there have been in the way people look at nature.

Three or four hundred years ago, for example, the ideal landscape in the eyes of educated people was a tamed, cleared and cultivated countryside. Bog and mountain and wild woodland were thought barbarous and horrible to look at. Man was the master of everything in creation and nature and its wildlife existed only for his benefit.

By the late 1700's and early 1800's, taste in landscape was changing. This began among sophisticated people who liked the wild and sublime scenery that some painters were now choosing. They were also reacting against the wholesale enclosures of land and the orderly geometry of agriculture. In literature, as well as painting, the new Romantic movement was putting aesthetic standards ahead of utilitarian ones. Now that fewer people were actually going hungry, bogs and mountains and waterfalls could be enjoyed for their untamed drama, their "picturesque" composition. So places like Connemara and its peasants received their first tourists.

A general change in popular taste had to wait for the Industrial Revolution and a reversal in traditional regard for the "civilizing" city. The new ugliness and overcrowding of the cities sent ordinary people out into the countryside to recuperate and enjoy their leisure. By the mid 19th century there was a boom in books about nature almost as dramatic as today's interest in wildlife films on television.

All this, of course, was far more true of England than of Ireland. With no Industrial Revolution to produce a reaction against the city, no large and respected class to lead changes in taste or thought, no distancing of urban people from the everyday uses of the land, Irish attitudes to nature remained utilitarian—what was it "good" for?

1

So, before the early 1900's and the growth of nationalist sentiment, the "inspirational" value of Ireland's bogland scarcely existed. To most Irish people, the bog was synonymous with hardship and the poorest way of life. When the poets of the new Ireland came to praise the native small farmer, they saw him as a vanquisher of nature—as when Padraic Colum, for example, extolled the ploughman as a "brute-tamer" urging on his horses:

"Earth savage, earth broken, the brutes, the dawn-man there in the sunset,
And the plough that is twin to the sword, that is founder of cities!"

The Irish had missed the reaction against industrial urban living that sent the English out to "wander lonely as a cloud" on their own boggy fells. But the romantic feelings of the new Irish nationalism tended to focus on the same sort of landscape. Among the bogs of the long-suffering Irish-speaking West, might be found the true soul of Ireland. So, at a time when most European painters were turning for inspiration to the cities, Irish artists such as James Humbert Craig were drawn to the great, windy skies and flowing landforms of Connemara. In Paul Henry's landscapes, too, which tidied up the bogland and its lakes into planes of luminous colour, people could enjoy a patriotic sort of beauty that hung calmly on the wall.

In modern Irish painting, the bog has kept its fascination for painters, but it often inspires a different set of feelings from the idyllic and pastoral ideas of half a century ago. In today's pictures, the bog is painted much more for itself: a primeval piece of nature with special powers to awe and impress—rather like the sea. In the Connemara landscapes of George Campbell, for example, the rough textures of rock and the untidy wetness of the moorland pools are used to create a solitary mood which is completely unsentimental. Patrick Collins, who spent his youth in Sligo, is another painter who has tried to put us in touch with the feelings of mystery and the sense of the ancient past, that walking the bogs can inspire. In his pictures, which may look so empty at first, there is the flash of bogland water, the gleam of sun along a dark horizon, the all-pervading moistness. At one point in his career, worried that his work was getting too gentle, he went off to dig ditches in Connemara to sharpen his eye again.

In Ulster, too, painters such as Colin Middleton and T.P. Flanagan have explored the sombre textures and rich, earthly colours of peatland to show its distinctive quality as

---

Plate 1 **Bog Inspiration**

1. *"Greater Butterwort on the Bog", County Kerry 1986. From a series of miniature water colours by Pauline Bewick. (Reproduced by kind permission of a private collector)*

2. *The sculptor Michael Casey at work, carving a free-form sculpture from Yew wood which was removed from a bog. (Reproduced by kind permission of the artist)*

3. *"West of Ireland Landscape" by James Humbert Craig. Oil on board. (Reproduced by kind permission of Allied Irish Banks plc)*

①

②

③

landscape. In his poem "Bogland", dedicated to Flanagan, Seamus Heaney gives another view of what makes the bogs so special:

"We have no prairies
To slice a big sun at evening —
Everywhere the eye concedes to
Encroaching horizon,
Is wooed into the cyclops' eye
Of a tarn. Or unfenced country
Is bog that keeps crusting
Between the sights of the sun."

You cannot conserve a whole landscape, of course, just to inspire poets and painters. But they are the spokesmen for our deeper feelings, and if we want to know what it is about bogland that can stir us so powerfully, we can find some of the clues among our works of art.

Figure 1 — "Under Mweelrea" by Michael Viney. A black and white pen and ink drawing of Mweelrea Mountain, County Mayo. (Reproduced by kind permission of the artist).

THE DISTRIBUTION AND FORMATION OF IRISH PEATLANDS

Peter Foss

Ireland is still in a position to boast a fine selection of oceanic peatlands of which there are three different types. These are fens, raised bogs and blanket bogs. There are two types of blanket bog, one occurs at low altitudes in the west of Ireland (Atlantic blanket bog) while the other is found in mountain ranges throughout the country (Mountain blanket bog).

Peat Formation

Peatlands are composed of deep layers of waterlogged peat and a surface layer of living vegetation. Peat consists of the dead remains of plants (and to a lesser extent of animals) that have accumulated over thousands of years. Peat accumulates in areas where the rate of plant production exceeds the rate of plant decomposition. Complete plant decomposition is prevented in areas where waterlogging occurs. In Ireland, high rainfall and low temperatures result in low evaporation which means that waterlogged soils are a common feature, for example in shallow basins. These waterlogged soils are anaerobic or poor in oxygen and oxygen is essential for the growth of the soil micro-organisms (bacteria and fungi) that bring about the complete breakdown of plant material. As a result of the poor microbial activity dead plants accumulate in waterlogged areas as peat.

Another factor which contributes to the accumulation of peat by preventing the growth of soil micro-organisms is the acidity of the ground water. In bogs, the acid nature of the ground water is produced by plants known as Bog Mosses, or *Sphagnum* species. These plants absorb the cations (positive ions) in rainwater (for example calcium and magnesium) and release hydrogen ions into the water. The more acidic the soil water, the less suitable it becomes for micro-organisms to grow and the plant remains therefore accumulate at a faster rate.

Distribution of Irish Peatland Types

Fens

The first peatland type is called a fen. Today, undamaged fens are rare in Ireland, due primarily to the effects of land reclamation. As a result they are rare in the Midlands, but they are still found in lowland areas in western Ireland. The black peat found in fens is formed from the remains of sedges and the "brown" fen mosses, which grow in alkaline (calcium-rich) conditions. This calcium-rich water is usually supplied to the fen by mineral-rich drainage water or springs. This is one of the major differences between fens and the other peatland types (Figure 2).

Raised Bogs

Raised bogs, also known as Ridge Raised bogs, High bogs, Red bogs and Raised Mires are found in the Midlands of Ireland. They are principally composed of moss peat, which is made up of the dead parts of the Bog Moss, *Sphagnum*. Raised bogs are the deepest of the Irish peatlands, for example at Raheenmore Bog, County Offaly the peat is 12m

PEATLAND TYPES

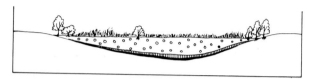

A. Fen

B. Raised Bog

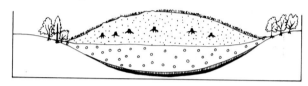

C. Blanket Bog

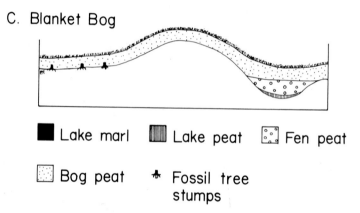

■ Lake marl   ▥ Lake peat   ⬚ Fen peat

⬚ Bog peat   ♣ Fossil tree stumps

Figure 2 — Transverse sections of Irish peatland types. Profile A shows fen, B shows raised bog and C shows blanket bog.

Plate 2 **Fen**

1. *Scragh Bog, County Westmeath in summer. The picture shows open water, sedge communities and fen carr. (Peter Foss)*

2. *Ragged Robin, a conspicuous species on Irish fens. (Office of Public Works)*

3. *Fly Orchid (Peter Foss)*

4. *Bog Bean in flower, usually found in the wetter areas on fens. (Gerry Doyle)*

5. *A sedge community on Pollardstown Fen, County Kildare in summer. Glaucous Sedge and Carnation Sedge are seen. (Peter Foss)*

deep. Raised bogs occur in places where the average rainfall is 800—900 mm per year. They get their name from the domed nature of the bog (Figure 2).

Blanket Bogs
Along the western seaboard of Ireland there are vast tracts of land covered in a carpet of peat of varying depth from 2—6 m. This peatland type is called Atlantic blanket bog although it is also known as Low level blanket bog and Western blanket bog. Unlike raised bogs the peat is composed of the dead remains of grasses and sedges and contains very little Bog Moss. The peat is usually dark brown to black in colour and is compact. It develops in areas where the average annual rainfall is greater than 1200 mm, and where rain falls on at least 235 days each year! (Figure 2).

Mountain blanket bog or High level blanket bog, forms a similar carpet in flat areas and on gentle slopes in mountain ranges throughout the country, above an elevation of 200m. The peat is also composed of dead grass or sedge material as is Atlantic blanket bog (Figure 2).

The History of Bog Development Trapped in Peat
The history of bog development is revealed by examining the different layers of peat exposed by turf cutters, since peat is composed of the remains of plants that grew on the surface of the bog. These plant remains are so well preserved that it is possible to identify them. Apart from the plant material present, peat as it accumulates traps the pollen produced by the bog plants which grew locally. By recording the pollen types and the numbers of grains produced by each species at different depths through the bog we can discover how the bog plants, and the abundance of each species, changed during the history of the bog. The peat also traps pollen blown in from the surrounding countryside. By examining these pollen types the history of the vegetation of Ireland has been elucidated (see also the chapter on Vegetation History).

Fen and Raised Bog History
Raised bog formation started at the end of the last glaciation—some 10,000 years ago— when the glaciers had retreated northwards. At this time much of central Ireland was covered by shallow lakes left behind by the melting ice. Lakes also formed where glacial ridges, such as eskers, impeded free drainage and trapped the water.

At the base of these shallow lakes there were deposits of lake marl overlying clay and glacial drift. These lakes were fed by mineral-rich groundwater and springs and supported floating plant communities, which sometimes produced a thin peat layer just above the lake marl. The lake edges were dominated by tall reed and sedge beds. As these plants died, their remains fell into the water and were only partly decomposed. They collected as peat on the lake bed. With time this process formed a thick layer of reed peat that rose towards the water surface. As the peat surface approached the upper water level, sedges invaded, and their remains added to the accumulating fen peat (Figure 3).

In time the fen peat layer in these shallow lakes became so thick (up to 2 m) that the roots of plants growing on the surface were no longer in contact with the calcium-rich ground water. When this happened the only source of minerals for the plants came from rainwater, a very poor source of the essential minerals needed for plant growth. As a

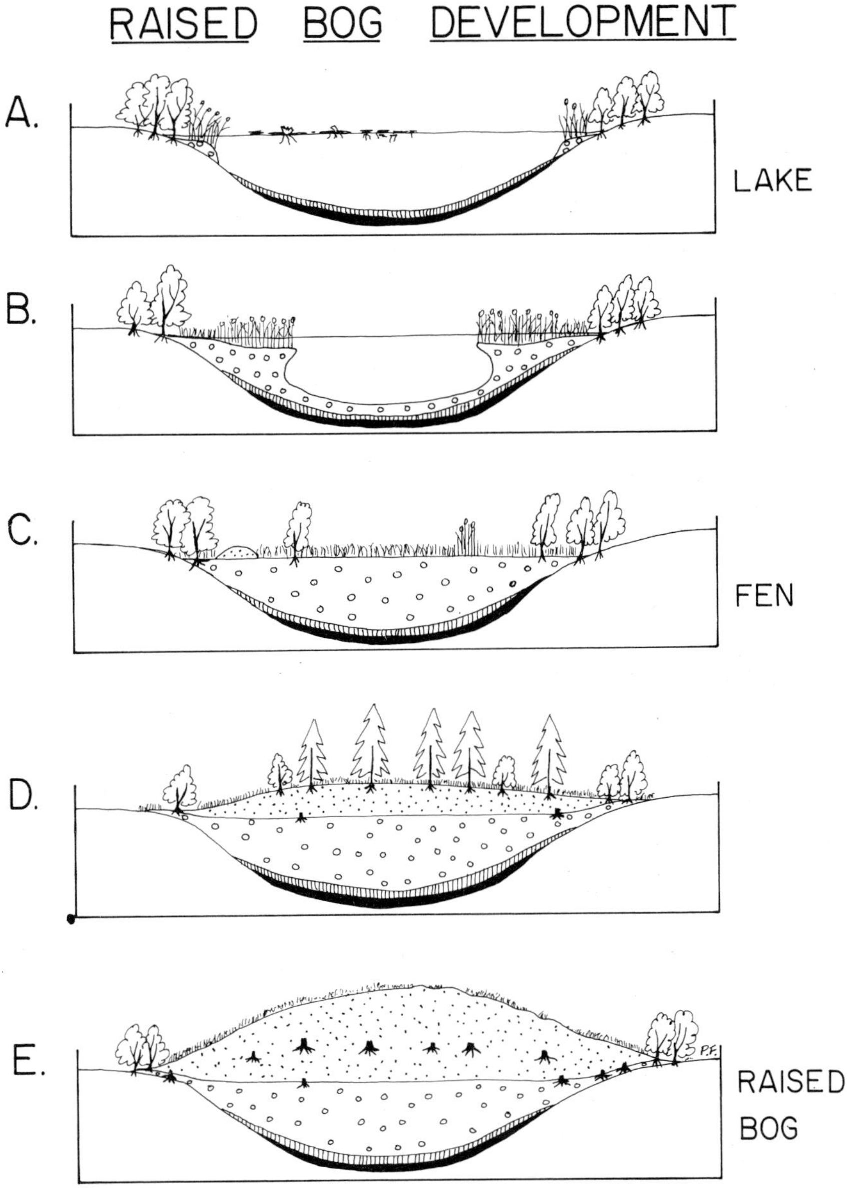

RAISED BOG DEVELOPMENT

Figure 3—The developmental stages from a lake to a raised bog. A represents a lake with an open body of water and marginal reedbeds. The lake has thin layers of marl and lake peat (for an explanation of the symbols, see previous figure). B represents a lake which is being infilled with fen reed peat. C is the fen stage. D is the raised bog woodland phase and E is a profile through a present raised showing a Pine stump layer buried in acid peat.

result plants invaded that were able to grow in the mineral-poor habitats on the surface of the peatland. The best indicator of the changing conditions was the invasion of the Bog Moss—*Sphagnum*. This moss became common in such transitional fen/bog habitats, and made the ground even more acid, by its ion exchange activity. This intermediate stage between fen and bog can be seen today at Scragh Bog, County Westmeath, where a mixture of lime loving fen plants and acid *Sphagnum* cushions grow together. Plants typical of raised bogs, such as Heathers, Sundews and Deer Sedge invaded the tops of the *Sphagnum* hummocks, completing the invasion of bog species.

The Bog Moss is important as it acts like a sponge or candle wick, drawing up water and keeping the surface of the bog wet and waterlogged, in all but the driest periods. So, even though the bog continued to grow upwards, away from the water table, the Bog Moss ensured that the water table rose in tandem with the rising peat level.

During the long history of bog growth, there have been occasional changes in the overall climate in Ireland. About 4,500 years ago the annual rainfall decreased. This caused bog surfaces to dry, and allowed the invasion and establishment of a Pine woodland on the surface of the bog. This woodland persisted for some 500 years, until the climate changed again and became wetter. Rapid bog growth recommenced as the surface became waterlogged, and the trees died. Tree stumps and whole tree trunks were buried and preserved in the rapidly accumulating *Sphagnum* peat (Figure 4). The layers of fen and *Sphagnum* peat and the buried Pine stumps are often seen exposed by turf cutters at the margins of raised bogs.

Blanket Bog History

Blanket bog formation in western Ireland also started at the end of the last glaciation, 10,000 years ago. Initially peat formation was confined to shallow lakes and wet hollows and an infilling sequence from open water to fen and acid peat is recorded in these areas. Later, acid peat spread out to form a blanket covering huge areas. While some spread may have taken place as early as 7,000 years ago, many areas were not engulfed until

---

Plate 3 **Raised Bogs**

1. *Hummock and pool system on Mongan Bog, County Offaly in September. The pools contain Bog Bean and are fringed by White Beak Sedge. (Brian Madden)*

2. *A Hare's nest hollowed out of a tall hummock of Cushion Moss. (Caitríona Douglas)*

3. *Cranberry on a hummock formed by Bog Moss and lichens. (Caitríona Douglas)*

4. *Soak system on Clara Bog, County Offaly. Note the open water surrounded by Soft Rush and the Birch trees further from the water. (Gerry Doyle)*

5. *Pitcher Plants on Mouds Bog, County Kildare in August. Note the red tinged pitcher-shaped leaves and the flowering heads. (Peter Foss)*

6. *Bog Moss hummock at the edge of a pool on a raised bog, topped by lichens and flowering Ling Heather in August. (Peter Foss)*

7. *A semi-aquatic variety of Bog Moss. (Peter Foss)*

4,000 years ago when the climate became wetter. Heavy rainfall caused minerals such as iron to be washed out or leached from the surface layers of the soil. These were deposited lower down where they formed an impermeable layer known as an iron pan. Water cannot move down through such a layer and the soil surface became waterlogged as a result. Under these conditions the accumulation and spread of peat was made possible.

Today in the west of Ireland the blanket bog rests directly on the stumps of Pine trees that were once part of extensive woodlands in the area and also covers large areas of farmland that were cultivated by Neolithic farmers (see the chapter on the Archaeology of Peatlands).

Figure 4—A Pine stump exposed in blanket bog by peat cutting. The stump is circa 4,000 years old. (Photograph courtesy of the Office of Public Works).

BOG VEGETATION

Catherine O'Connell

There are a number of plants that are commonly found on all Irish bogs. This core of species includes Ling Heather, Cross-leaved Heath, Bog Cotton, Sundew, Bog Bean, Bog Asphodel, White Beak Sedge and a number of Bog Mosses or *Sphagnum* species. Many of these plants and mosses are especially adapted to living in mineral-poor, waterlogged, acid habitats. The common and scientific names of the species likely to be encountered on Irish bogs are listed in Appendix 1.

Carnivorous or Insectivorous Bog Plants

Some bog plants have overcome the difficulty of obtaining nitrogen and phosphorus in an unique way. They eat animals! These carnivorous plants employ two methods of catching their prey. The Sundews and Butterworts produce sticky substances that act like fly paper, while the Bladderworts and the Pitcher Plant trap their prey.

There are three species of Sundew found on Irish bogs. The leaves of these plants are spoon-shaped. The surface of the "spoon" is covered with tiny tentacles that are topped with a drop of sticky fluid. Insects are trapped among the tentacles, which bend and enclose them. The whole leaf folds over like a clenched fist as the insect is digested for its nutrients.

The leaves of Butterworts are bright yellow-green and sticky. Insects stuck on the surface are digested by chemicals produced by the plant.

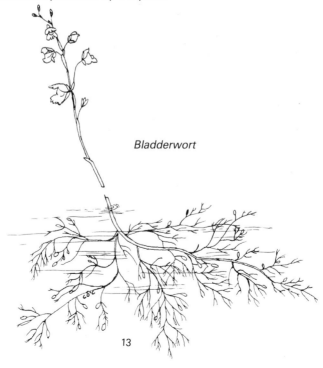

Bladderwort

The Bladderworts are found in bog pools and have submerged leaves bearing tiny bladders that are used to trap insects. To accomplish this a bladder is fitted with a trap door and a trigger hair. When the prey touches the trigger hair, the door opens, releasing the partial vacuum within and sucking in the animal with a drop of water. In an instant the door shuts on the victim, which is subsequently digested.

In 1906 the conspicuous Pitcher Plant was introduced to Ireland from Canada. It was planted on a raised bog in County Roscommon. Since then it has been transplanted onto a number of bogs, and survives today on four raised bogs and at one site on Atlantic blanket bog. The reddish leaves of the plant are pitcher-shaped and hold water. Hairs on the upper part of the pitcher are directed downwards allowing insects to crawl into the pitcher but presenting an obstruction to their escape. As a result the insects drown and are digested in the enzyme-rich fluid.

Raised Bog Vegetation

The living surface of a raised bog is made up of a mosaic of pools, lawns and hummocks. The most important plant on raised bogs is *Sphagnum* or the Bog Moss, of which there are ten species commonly found. Some *Sphagnum* species grow quickly, forming hummocks, while others are found floating in the pools. It is possible to distinguish different species by their colour and by the habitat in which they are found. Green species are found in pools; red, copper and yellow species form the lawns; brown, orange and different green species form the hummocks. Together they form a colourful background through which the other bog plants grow.

Bog Rosemary

In the pools the emergent tri-lobed leaf of the Bog Bean is unmistakable. Two of the insectivorous plants are found here, the Sundew and the submerged Bladderwort. The yellow flower heads of the Bladderwort emerge from the water during the summer. Sometimes in shallower pools Brown Beak Sedge may be found.

Around the edges of the pools and on the lawns the White Beak Sedge forms a distinct band, intermingled with Bog Cotton and the yellow lily-like flowering heads of the Bog Asphodel. Near the drier margins of the bog some pools only fill up with water after heavy rain. When these are dry they have a pale grey-green layer of algae in their bases and may contain Bog Cotton.

Plate 4 **Raised Bogs**
1. *General view of the dome of a raised bog at Mouds Bog, County Kildare in August. The brighter patches are White Beak Sedge. (Peter Foss)*
2. *Four-spotted Chaser Dragonfly resting on Ling Heather on Clara Bog, County Offaly. (Paul Portelli)*
3. *A hummock-forming Bog Moss and Round-leaved Sundew. (Caitríona Douglas)*
4. *A hummock and pool system on a raised bog in August when Ling Heather is in flower. (Peter Foss)*
5. *"Sausage peat" or Difco machine in operation. (Andy Cole)*
6. *A Snipe's nest on the surface of a Raised bog containing four eggs. (Caitríona Douglas)*
7. *The leaf of the Long-leaved Sundew which has trapped an unsuspecting fly, using the sticky fluid on the tentacles. (Office of Public Works).*

The hummocks are the driest places on the bog. On their tops, Ling Heather bushes sometimes up to thirty years old are found if the bog is unburned. The stems of these older bushes are often encrusted with a grey layer of lichens. Cross-leaved Heath, Bog Rosemary, Deer Sedge and Bog Cotton emerging from a rich mat of ground lichens are common here. Sometimes very large hummocks up to one metre tall are encountered. These are formed not by *Sphagnum* but by the bright green compact Cushion Moss. The tops of such hummocks are often colonised by mosses typical of woodlands as well as a selection of lichens, mainly *Cladonia* species. Branched, cup-like and matchstick-like forms of *Cladonia* are found.

On larger hummocks among the heather and on the lawns formed by the Bog Moss, the leaves and wine-red berries of the Cranberry may be seen.

Cutaway areas, where peat has been hand-cut for centuries, surround most of the remaining raised bogs. These areas are drier and consequently present a contrasting variety of plants and animals to those found on the waterlogged bog surface. Apart from the bog species mentioned above, many weeds, grasses, ferns, bushes and trees occur in cutaway bog. On the dry bog edge adjacent to the cutaway, large shrinkage cracks can often be seen in the peat.

Atlantic Blanket Bog Vegetation

The vegetation of Atlantic blanket bog contains many of the species commonly found on raised bogs but there are some important differences. For example two of the Ericoid shrubs, Bog Rosemary and Cranberry, that are typical of raised bogs, are absent from Atlantic blanket bog. The appearance of Atlantic blanket bog vegetation is different because it is dominated by grass and sedge species and not by a mixture of shrub, sedge and mosses as we saw in the case of raised bogs. The dominant species in Atlantic blanket bog include Purple Moor Grass, Black Bog Rush, Bog Cotton and Deer Sedge. The bog is a golden-brown colour in winter. This is due to the fact that as the sedges and grasses die back, particularly Purple Moor Grass and Bog Cotton, their leaves take on a golden-brown colour.

The Black Bog Rush is an unexpected plant in this habitat. It is a species typically found in fen vegetation in the rest of Europe! Its presence on Atlantic blanket bog in western Ireland is thought to be influenced by westerly winds which bring in minerals derived from sea spray. The presence of this plant in Atlantic blanket bog never ceases to puzzle botanists who have suggested many other reasons to explain its occurrence here.

Purple Moor Grass

During the winter there is a layer of jelly-like slime made up of algae, sometimes up to ten centimetres thick on the surface of Atlantic blanket bog especially in waterlogged areas. If this material dries in summer it forms a crisp mat, ensuring moist conditions at the peat surface. *Sphagnum* is not abundant in such waterlogged areas. A red wormlike plant (a liverwort) and a black moss, are characteristic plants widely distributed on the bog surface. In areas that are not so waterlogged, hummocks formed by *Sphagnum* and Silver-haired Moss are found. These may be surrounded by winding *Sphagnum* pools.

While sedges and grasses dominate Atlantic blanket bog, other plants such as Milkwort, Tormentil, Lousewort, Carnation Sedge, and the insectivorous Lusitanian Butterwort are found. The Cross-leaved Heath and Ling Heather are here also but they rarely form large bushes as they do on raised bogs. The dwarf habit of these shrubs on Atlantic blanket bog results from the effects of frequent burning, grazing and permanent surface waterlogging. In Connemara and Donegal, Mackay's Heath is encountered occasionally on the blanket bog.

There are numerous pools similar to those found on raised bogs on the surface of blanket bogs. There are also larger lakes: in Mayo these have a peat base and contain Bog Bean, American Pipewort and Water Lobelia, while in Connemara the lake bottoms reach mineral soil and in addition to the above species contain Common Reed, Pondweed, Yellow Water-lily and White Water-lily.

There are islands in some of the larger bog lakes which are protected by the surrounding water from fire and grazing and are better drained. On these islands substantial bushes of Ling Heather and Cross-leaved Heath and lichens are abundant, along with other plants which are not found on the open bog surface. Crowberry and Juniper are occasionally found on these islands. The islands found in lakes in the blanket bog in Connemara are often wooded. Trees such as Holly, Oak, Yew, Willow and Scot's Pine survive in such habitats.

Mountain Blanket Bog Vegetation

Mountain blanket bog contains many of the species found on the other two bog types. Hummocks of *Sphagnum* and Silver-haired Moss are found with abundant lichens on them, surrounded by *Sphagnum* pools. There are occasional lakes. Mountain blanket bog occurs in colder and humid or "damp" uplands and mountain environments. Species associated with such mountain habitats include Crowberry, Bilberry and Clubmoss. The Cloudberry, a plant typical of bogs in the colder parts of Northern Europe, is only found in Ireland on mountain blanket bog in the Sperrin Mountains, County Tyrone.

Beak Sedge

Ling Heather, Cross-leaved Heath and Bog Rosemary are common. Within the bog lakes floating *Sphagnum* species, Bog Bean and Bottle Sedge are found. Around the lake edges, Bog Asphodel, Bog Cotton and White Beak Sedge generally form a neat fringe.

Drainage Features of Peatlands

The raised and blanket bogs described are mineral-poor habitats because they are fed solely by rainfall. Much of the rainwater collects on, or is held close to the surface of the bog through the sponge-like action of *Sphagnum*, but a considerable amount of water runs off the bog surface either directly or through an internal drainage system within a bog. On raised bogs the usual drainage system is a "soak", while on blanket bogs, a system of surface drains lead to swallow holes (entrances to underground drains). These drainage structures are easily distinguished and are fed by moving water which continually passes through them. The additional nutrient inputs are reflected in the presence of numerous plants that are not found on the acid bog surface. In Appendix 2, a list of the species typical of these drainage features can be found.

Soak systems

Clara bog in County Offaly is the only Irish raised bog that still has a well developed soak system. The soak consists of a series of lakes, interconnected by natural drains with an exit drain leading to the bog margin. The lake water is rich in minerals as it is being fed continuously by springs rising beneath the peat mass.

The open water is fringed by Marsh Pennywort, Bottle Sedge, Soft Rush, White Sedge, Bog Bean, Mud Sedge, Bog Cotton, Bulrush, Marsh Cinquefoil, Angelica, Devil's Bit Scabious, Marsh Orchid, Royal Fern, Yorkshire Fog, Sweet Vernal Grass, Bent Grass and Sharp-flowered Rush. There are also a number of mosses typical of mineral-rich conditions.

Behind the marsh zone there is a shrub-dominated area, where Crowberry and Cranberry are found, and further from the lake a swampy Birch woodland, with Birch, Willow, Bilberry, Brambles, Bog Myrtle, Broad Buckler-fern and Purple Moor Grass. The Birch trees support a rich epiphytic lichen and moss flora on their barks. In the ground layer *Sphagnum* species, typical of less acidic conditions, and Common Hair Moss are found.

The Rannoch Rush *(Scheuchzeria palustris)* was found in an extensive soak system on Pollagh bog in County Offaly. This was the only Irish station for the plant. Sadly, the bog was developed by Bord na Móna in the 1950's and the plant is now extinct in this country.

The drains between lakes in the soak system are marked out by a series of strips or patches of vegetation quite different to that of the raised bog surface. They contain Purple Moor Grass, Soft Rush, Crowberry and often abundant stands of the fragrant Bog Myrtle.

Swallow holes and drains

Within blanket bogs drainage features include swallow holes and surface drains. Swallow holes are steep-sided holes leading to underground water channels in which water movement can be heard. On the well-drained peat surrounding a swallow hole there are large bushes of Bell Heather, Ling Heather and Cross-leaved Heath. In the base and on the sides of the hole, many woodland plants including ferns and mosses enjoy a sheltered habitat. These include Honeysuckle, Brambles, Tormentil, Soft Rush, Heath Bedstraw, grasses and several ferns including Bracken, Hay-scented Buckler-fern, Royal Fern and Hard Fern.

Natural surface drains occur on blanket bog. These channel water from the surrounding area to deep drains that run over the mineral soil. These mineral-rich deep drains contain sedge and marsh plant communities. Numerous sedges such as the Mud, Carnation, Bottle and Greater Tussock Sedges are found together with Mare's Tail, Marsh Pennywort, Marsh Cinquefoil, Spotted Orchid, Water Horsetail and the Soft and Toad Rushes. The plant communities in these drains often form mats of floating vegetation similar to fen communities.

FEN VEGETATION

Catherine O'Connell

Extensive areas of rich fen vegetation were common in Ireland about 7,500 years ago. These fens are preserved as peat under the bogs. Today there are only a few large fens still intact. The vegetation of these areas is rich in plant species for two reasons. Firstly, the fen is continuously fed by spring water which is rich in minerals, especially lime. This means that the peat substrate is alkaline. Secondly, a number of distinct habitats are found within some fens: these range from areas of open water fringed by sedge and marsh plants to areas of fen woodland, also known as "fen carr". As the habitat is varied, up to two hundred different plants can be found on Irish fens. The common and scientific names of the plants likely to be encountered on fens are listed in Appendix 3.

The wooded areas on a fen are the driest parts. In the areas where sedge and marsh species dominate, the ground is soft and quaking and there is usually abundant surface water all year round. This vegetation is fragile and a group of people or animals crossing a fen can cause considerable damage which takes a long time to repair.

Fen vegetation is light brown in appearance for most of the year. This is due to the presence of standing dead parts of the typical plants and a thick carpet of lime-loving mosses, known as the "brown mosses", some of which are quite rare in Ireland. These mosses are often coated with white lime from the mineral-rich water in which they grow.

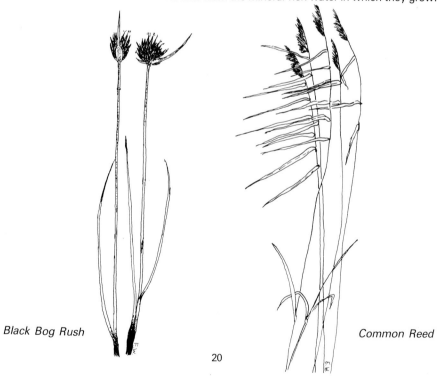

Black Bog Rush

Common Reed

Besides the mosses, plants dominating the surface of the fen include grasses and sedges. The most obvious of these are the Saw Sedge, Black Bog Rush, Common Reed and Purple Moor Grass. The Saw Sedge, as the name suggests, has leaves with sharp edges that can cut paper (and hands !). This plant tends to form patches on the fen. The Black Bog Rush forms pronounced clumps or tussocks between which the brown fen mosses are found. The Common Reed, the tallest Irish grass, forms patches especially in drains running through fens. Intermingled with these are a number of typical fen plants such as Fen Rush, Hemp Agrimony, Angelica, Fen Thistle, Fen Bog Cotton and Fen Sedge. There are also insectivorous plants, such as, Butterworts and Bladderworts, and a number of Orchids, some of which are rare species in Ireland. These include Marsh Orchid, Fly Orchid and Fragrant Orchid.

Fen Rush   *Saw Sedge*

A closer examination of the various habitats on a fen reveals the diversity of plant species found there. Many aquatic plants flourish in the slow moving or still waters of the fen including Duckweed, Pondweed and Stonewort.

Perhaps the most interesting places on fens are the quaking areas in which sedge and marsh plants are found. As many as fifteen different sedge species can be distinguished. These include the Fen, Mud, Bottle, Flea, Slender, Yellow, Soft and White Sedges. Many marsh and wet meadow species are found. The most common ones include the Bog Bean, Horsetail, Marsh Cinquefoil, Meadowsweet, Devil's Bit Scabious, Willow Herb, Fen Thistle, Marsh Bedstraw, Wild Valerian, Lesser Spearwort, Mint, Lady's Smock, Blackhead and Red Rattle.

The wooded areas or fen carr support mainly Willow, Alder and Birch trees. The shade provided by the trees allows woodland mosses and ferns to grow. On one Irish fen, Scragh bog, Wintergreen is found in such shaded woodland conditions.

Fens are habitats which are constantly changing. Part of their natural growth and development involves a gradual replacement of the fen plant communities with groups of plants more typical of mineral-poor, acid conditions. On some Irish fens the first stages in this process are apparent. It is possible to find lime-loving plants growing side by side with plants which enjoy more acid conditions. Hummocks of Bog Moss *(Sphagnum)* are colonised by bog species such as Ling Heather, Cross-leaved Heath, Bog Cotton, Sundew and Cranberry.

Fen Thistle

THE FAUNA OF BOGS

Brian Madden

Although bogs might at first glance appear unattractive to wildlife, there are a large number of animals that have successfully adapted to life in this unique habitat. Many of the animals occur at low densities and one may have to walk over a large area of bog before seeing a bird or mammal. Others are small and inconspicuous and have to be hunted for with a hand lens. Various animals are associated with one or other of the different types of bogs. Even within a bog, different groups of animals are found in the various habitats, such as hummocks, lawns and pools. A list of some of the typical bog animals is given in Appendix 4. There are numerous insect species found on bogs and these animals will be dealt with in a subsequent chapter.

Molluscs

Snails and slugs occur on blanket bog but are rare on raised bogs, although the Large Black Slug is common on all bog types.

Slug

Amphibians

The Common Frog is very well adapted to living on bogs and occurs on all of our bog types. It is an important predator feeding on the more active arthropods such as Beetles, Spiders and Bugs. Frogs come out of hibernation during March. Shortly afterwards they mate and the female lays masses of eggs in the drains found in the cutaway area of bogs and sometimes in bog pools. The tadpoles take about ten weeks to develop into tiny frogs after which they can leave the water and move onto the general bog surface.

Reptiles

The Common Lizard or the Viviparous Lizard is occasionally seen on hot days basking on rocks or on hummocks of Bog Moss in blanket bogs. This is the only species of Lizard found in Ireland and it occurs in other habitats besides bogs. The Viviparous Lizard gets its name from the fact that the female retains the eggs in her body until they are fully developed and ready to hatch. The living young are produced in summer and are active within a few minutes after birth. This species feeds on Spiders and various insects such as Flies, Beetles, Ants and Moths, all of which are found on blanket bogs.

Birds

The density and diversity of bird species on bogs is relatively low in comparison to woodlands or estuaries. Many of the species which do occur on bogs, particularly birds of prey and waders, are species which require large expanses of open space for breeding purposes. Some of these birds are very scarce breeding species in Ireland, others are only summer visitors to bogs.

The Red Grouse is the most characteristic species of bogs. Although it is widely distributed it is usually difficult to see, because of its secretive nature. Grouse feed almost entirely on Ling Heather and actively select the young shoots which are a more nutritious food source. They also require mature Ling Heather bushes for nesting and shelter.

The Golden Plover is one of the most typical birds of bogs. It has, however, become less widespread throughout its European breeding range during this century, and in Ireland it only breeds in small numbers on blanket bogs in the west and north of Ireland. The observer who enters a breeding territory may be lucky to spot one of the birds as it stands guard in a prominent position. The breeding grounds are vacated usually by mid-July.

Snipe

The Snipe, Meadow Pipit, Skylark and Hooded Crow are the commonest birds of bogs. The Curlew breeds quite widely on both raised and blanket bog. Most of the breeding Curlews return to the nesting grounds early in the year, many by February to the raised bogs, although mountain blanket bogs are not occupied until April. The parents are most conspicuous during courtship early in the season and later when the young are present. By late-July, most of the breeding grounds have been vacated.

The Mallard and Teal breed on bogs and both are widely distributed. The Raven is a very characteristic species of mountain blanket bogs.

The Peregrine Falcon is a species of mountain blanket bog and requires large areas of open terrain for hunting purposes. The Merlin and the Hen Harrier are very scarce breeding species associated with both raised and blanket bogs. They may nest in dry Ling Heather or amongst low scrub adjacent to the bog. Like the Peregrine they require large expanses of open areas for hunting. The Kestrel is the commonest bird of prey found on peatlands and is often seen hovering over the bog in search of prey.

Bogs were formerly the natural habitat of the Greenland White-fronted Goose, which was traditionally known as the "bog goose". The Geese breed in Greenland but spend the winter in Ireland and Scotland. Bogs can provide all the birds' needs in terms of food and safe roosting sites. The birds feed on the green shoots and the roots of White Beak Sedge and Bog Cotton. The Geese may still be seen in their natural habitat on Atlantic blanket bogs in the west of Ireland in areas such as the Bangor Erris peninsula in north-west Mayo. In the Midlands, the feeding grounds for the Geese are areas such as callows, turloughs, farmland and improved grasslands along rivers particularly the Shannon and the Little Brosna. The birds tend to use the raised bogs adjacent as areas into which they retreat if they are disturbed from the feeding grounds. In recent decades there has been a decline in the winter population. This is linked with the disappearance

Greenland White-Fronted Goose

of bogs. Today the bulk of the population winter on the Wildfowl Reserve in County Wexford where they feed on managed grassland, stubble and winter cereals.

Several other bird species occur on bogs but also require shrubs, low trees or rocks for perching posts. These include the Linnet, Stonechat, Whinchat, Wheatear and Cuckoo. The last three species are only summer visitors to Ireland.

Mammals

The Irish Hare is the only common and readily seen mammal on all bogs. Regular pathways used by the hares, known as "hare runs", are often a conspicuous feature of the bog surface, as are "hare nests" which are dug out of the larger hummocks on the bog surface. These nests shelter the Hare in an otherwise exposed habitat.

Pygmy Shrew

25

Native Red Deer occur in Killarney National Park where they roam large areas of mountain blanket bog. Native stock have recently been introduced to Connemara National Park. Red Deer, though not of native stock also occur in Glenveagh National Park and in the Wicklow Mountains. Although deer are large animals they are usually very secretive and difficult to find.

Red Deer

Fox

Feral Goats occur in small numbers in the most remote areas of mountain blanket bogs. The Fox, Otter and Pygmy Shrew occasionally visit bogs. The Fox and the Otter are sometimes seen crossing bogs on their way to hunting grounds.

THE FAUNA OF FENS

Brian Madden

A larger number of animals inhabit fens than bogs because of the greater diversity of habitat and the richer vegetation found on fens. The various habitats on the fen support different animal communities. These habitats include areas of open water and marginal ditches, the quaking areas where the sedge and marsh plants occur and the wooded areas. A list of some of the animals likely to be encountered on fens is given in Appendix 4. Insects are abundant on fens and the various species found will be discussed in a subsequent chapter.

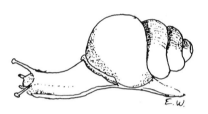

Water Snail

Molluscs

Snails are numerous on fens because of the high calcium content of the water in these habitats which provides the calcium necessary to allow the secretion of their shells. Several rare species occur within the Saw Sedge community including *Vertigo geyeri* which is normally found in Scandinavia and the Alps, but this species is usually difficult to find and is only recognised by an expert. It occurs on Pollardstown fen.

Fish

Two species of Stickleback occur in the alkaline waters of fens, the Three-spined Stickleback and the Ten-spined Stickleback. The Three-spined Stickleback is the commonest species, and forms an important part of the diet of the Grey Heron and the Otter. The Sticklebacks are carnivorous fish and feed on the wide range of invertebrates that occur in fens. They are found in shallow water where there are areas of emergent or submerged rooted vegetation.

Amphibians

The Common Newt, Ireland's only newt, occurs on fens. Newts live on dry land outside the breeding season but they must return to water to breed. During the breeding season the male is readily distinguishable from the female by the presence of a continuous wavy crest which runs the length of the body. The female lays her eggs singly on the leaves of the submerged aquatic plants found on fens. When the eggs hatch the newt tadpole is more fish-like than that of the frog. By the end of the summer the young newt crawls out of the water and seeks shelter under vegetation. When on land newts feed on Earthworms, Slugs and Insects

Common Frog

while in water they prey on aquatic larvae, molluscs, Frog spawn and tadpoles. Like Frogs, Newts hibernate during the winter. The Common Frog is also found in fens. Like the Newt, the life cycle of this species takes place in different habitats on the fen.

Birds

Fens provide breeding sites and feeding areas for a wide variety of birds. On Pollardstown fen twenty-seven different species of birds have been found breeding on or in the immediate vicinity of the fen. The stands of Saw Sedge and the Reedbeds are ideal habitats for many species in spring and summer. The Little Grebe, Great Crested Grebe, Mute Swan, Teal, Mallard, Water Rail, Moorhen and Coot all breed within this area. The nests are built safely above the water level, but occasionally they are flooded if the water table rises. The Sedge Warbler and the Reed Bunting also breed in this area but they build their nests high up in the Reeds well above the water level. These species avail of the large supply of insects found on fens to feed their young.

In the wet marshy ground of the fen the Lapwing and Snipe breed. The Lapwing is a very conspicuous bird and as one approaches the nest it will attempt to mob the intruder while uttering loud "peewit" cries.

The Stonechat and its close relative the Whinchat, which is a summer visitor, nest in the marginal areas of the fen and frequently use plants such as the Saw Sedge and the Common Reed as song posts. The Skylark and the Meadow Pipit are also common breeding species of fens.

Fen carr is an ideal breeding habitat for many common passerines (perching and songbirds) such as Wren, Dunnock, Robin, Blackbird and Song Thrush. During the summer, Birch and Willow trees attract good numbers of Willow Warblers and Chiffchaffs. Other species which may breed within fens include Cuckoo, Wheatear, Grasshopper Warbler, Whitethroat and Spotted Flycatcher. The Bittern formerly bred in fens in Ireland but is now sadly extinct as a breeding species and is only a very rare visitor to this country.

In late summer and autumn large numbers of Swallows, House Martins and Sand Martins may be seen hawking over the fens in search of insects. At dusk these birds settle to roost in the Reed and Saw Sedge communities for the night.

During autumn and winter substantial numbers of wildfowl occur on fens if there is an adequate area of open water. Wigeon, Shoveler, Tufted Duck and Pochard are common species. Whooper Swans, Gadwall, Pintail and Goldeneye may also occur. Grey Herons are frequent visitors to fens during autumn and winter. Golden Plover, Lapwing, Curlew, Redshank and Snipe are all common waders which occur in the wetter areas of the fen during winter.

Birds of prey are attracted to fens because of the plentiful supply of small birds and other prey. The Kestrel and Sparrowhawk are the commonest species and may nest close to the fen. A visiting Hen Harrier will quickly put to flight all the small birds of the area as it "quarters" the fen in search of an unsuspecting victim. The Peregrine and Merlin are occasional visitors to fens.

During winter flocks of finches occur in the fen carr. Chaffinches, Greenfinches and Linnets are common while Goldfinches, Redpolls and Brambling may also be seen.

Mammals

Mammals are uncommon on fens although several species do visit them. The Otter is the most frequently encountered mammal. It is largely nocturnal but may occasionally be seen by day swimming in areas of open water or scurrying along ditches. Otters are fierce hunters and although they feed chiefly on fish they will also take frogs, small mammals, birds and even invertebrates.

Otter

The North American Mink is another mammal which visits fens. It was introduced to Ireland for fur-farming in the 1950's but since then some have escaped from captivity and have found a niche in the wild. This species has been seen regularly at Pollardstown fen in County Kildare. The Mink resembles the Otter in appearance and behaviour but tends to be a more vicious predator. The Fox, Pygmy Shrew and Rabbit are other visitors to fens.

INSECTS OF PEATLANDS

Martin Speight and Brian Madden

To some, any mention of the insects of bog and fen conjures up visions of being eaten alive by blood-sucking Horse-flies and Midges. In reality, Midges and Horse-flies are only a nuisance for a restricted season. There are few species of Horse-fly in Ireland and those species occurring on fens and bogs rarely worry man. The largest Horse-fly, found only on sheltered bogs in Ireland is very scarce in most of western Europe. The smallest Irish Horse-fly is also our rarest and is found only on two or three fens. This species is black in colour but its eyes are marked in swirling patterns of gold. Many of the insects found on bogs and fens have developmental stages that are aquatic and which are found in pools, while the adults are free-flying. Examples are Dragonflies, Horse-flies, non-biting Midges and Water Beetles. A list of some of the insects and other invertebrates likely to be encountered in peatlands is given in Appendix 5.

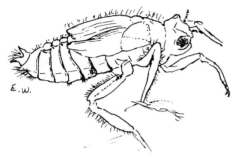

Dragonfly Nymph

Bogs

Bogs are unattractive habitats for insects for a number of reasons. These include fluctuating water levels, seasonal food scarcity, a lack of over-wintering sites safely above the winter high-water level, exposure to wind, low temperatures and deoxygenated ground water. The build up of peat which characterises these habitats, demonstrates how inhospitable they are. In other habitats it is the insects and other invertebrates that begin to process the dead plant material for recycling through the ecosystem.

Flying insects such as Horse-flies have managed to escape, to some extent, the limitations on food supply in bogs. As adults, the Horse-flies can move into fields adjacent to the bog and obtain a good protein meal from the blood of cattle or other domestic stock. Less mobile organisms have to make do with what the bog has to offer. Not surprisingly, there are few insects that are characteristic of bogs and found only there.

The Butterflies and Moths are the most conspicuous group of insects that a visitor will encounter on bogs. The Large Heath is the only Butterfly confined to peatlands. It is widely distributed in Ireland in such habitats. This Butterfly is difficult to approach but it may be recognised at a distance by its characteristic zig-zag flight pattern always near the bog surface. Most of the other Butterflies and Moths found on bogs such as the Green Hairstreak, the Meadow Brown and the Small Tortoiseshell also occur in other habitats. There are many more species of Moths than Butterflies on bogs. For example on Mongan bog one hundred and thirty-eight species have been recorded. The Emperor Moth, the Buff Ermine, the Large Yellow Underwing, the Oak Eggar and the Fox Moth are just some of the more prominent bog species. Caterpillars of some of these species are commonly seen on the bogs in summer and autumn. Many are large, brightly coloured and hairy. The empty brown, silk, pupal cases of the Emperor Moth and Oak Eggar are often found among Ling Heather on raised bogs.

Dragonflies and Damselflies are the aerial hunters on bogs during summer. Dragonflies are strong fliers and the rustling of their wings as they swoop about hunting may be heard from quite a distance away. The Four-spotted Chaser, a large brown species, and the Black Darter are common. Damselflies are more delicate insects and have a more delicate flight pattern. The metallic green body of the Emerald Damselfly and the brilliant red of the Large Red Damselfly make them very conspicuous against the bog vegetation.

Large Heath

One of the few conspicuous "terrestrial" insects encountered in Ireland only in bogs, is the Large Marsh Grasshopper. This beautiful orange, green and black insect, a common variety of which is actually purple in colour, is the largest Irish grasshopper and is at the northern edge of its range here. It occurs only at very low altitude in very sheltered bogs.

The most characteristic insects of peatlands are some of the species which inhabit bog pools. In the unpolluted, mineral-poor and cool conditions of the bog pool a number of insects with a predominantly northern European distribution are found.

Some interesting insects are found in areas dominated by Birch trees on Irish bogs. The rotting wood of these trees supports species such as the large and now internationally threatened Cranefly, *Dictaenidia bimaculata*.

The cutaway areas around the margins of bogs support a more diverse fauna than the bog itself. The species found here include the "bearded" Scathophagid Fly and the Red-banded Sawfly which inhabit areas dominated by plants such as Horsetails. These areas are well worth a visit in addition to the bog proper for anyone with an interest in seeing a variety of insects and allied organisms in Ireland.

Fens

Fens, in contrast to bogs support greater numbers of insects not found in other habitats. The higher nutrient status and the greater availability of over-wintering sites are partly responsible. The old stems of Bulrush, especially those that have been tunnelled out by the caterpillars of the

Emperor Moth

Bulrush Wainscot Moth, are like multi-storey tenement blocks for insects and other small animals that require hibernation sites. Flies, Beetles, Spiders, Ichneumen Wasps and various other tenants can all be found crammed into these stems in winter. Alternative retreats are provided by the bark crannies of Willow and Alder on sites where fen woodland or fen carr has developed.

The adult of the Cigar Gall Fly is rarely seen although the elongate stem-galls caused by the larvae of this species may be found on the stems of the Common Reed.

In Ireland, fen carr supports its own group of characteristic insects. These include Ireland's largest and one of our most magnificent Long-horn Beetles, the purple and bronze Musk Beetle. The larvae of the Musk Beetle consume the dead wood of Willow and Alder trunks.

A casual visitor will encounter a profusion of insects in the different habitats on the fen. The aquatic larvae of Caddis and Mayflies feed mainly on plant fragments. The larvae of Dragonflies and Damselflies and many species of Beetle are carnivorous and inhabit the pools. The free-flying adults of the Mayflies, Dragonflies and Damselflies are common throughout the summer.

The most obvious insects are the Butterflies. Most of the common Irish species occur including the Speckled Wood, the Meadow Brown, the Ringlet, the Small Heath, the Small Copper, the Common Blue, the Peacock and the Small Tortoiseshell. Two rarer Butterflies, the Wood White and the Brimstone are regular visitors to fens although neither of them breed here. The Brimstone, which overwinters as an adult, is one of the earliest Butterflies to emerge in spring and may be seen on the wing as early as March. A Butterfly of particular note which breeds on fens is the Marsh Fritillary. It is an uncommon and locally distributed species in Ireland and Europe. The foodplant of this species is the Devil's Bit Scabious which is common on fens.

Small Copper

Is a casual visit to an Irish bog or fen likely to give rise to an encounter with any of the rather special elements of the Irish fauna mentioned in the previous pages? Certainly on a sunny day between May and September Butterflies and Dragonflies are likely to be seen, but only a specialist would recognise whether the north European Dragonfly were among them. A few Horse-flies will probably come to greet you, but only the privileged are likely to be bitten by a rarity. A Water Beetle moving in the depths of a bog pool may be a rare species from northern Europe but it may also be a common species.

The sharp-sighted are likely to catch a glimpse of the largest Irish Spider, running over Bog Moss before plunging full tilt into the bog pool, and wonder why that spectacular little animal has not been mentioned in these pages. Similarly plants such as Angelica in flower beside the bog are likely to carry an enormous, blue-black fussy-looking Tachinid Fly, whose larvae parasitise those of the Fox Moth. Why is this fly not mentioned? Both of these animals occur in a wide range of vegetation types in Ireland. Here an attempt has been made to highlight species that are characteristic of bog and fen. Even though bog and fen faunas are limited in comparison with what can be found in a woodland, they still comprise hundreds of insect species and diverse representatives of other invertebrate groups such as Mites and Spiders. These few pages are inadequate to do justice to even those few species which have been mentioned. Go, see for yourself. No words can adequately encapsulate the glory of a Dragonfly in flight or the subtlety of a Moth's colours. But take care, wherever you tread is the home of some small animal, unseen but present.

Plate 5 **Atlantic Blanket Bog**

1. *Derrybeg Bog in the Glenveagh National Park, County Donegal. The bog is scenically located behind the sandy beach at the head of Lough Veagh. (Office of Public Works).*

2. *A White Water-lily growing in a bog lake in Atlantic Blanket Bog. (Gerry Doyle)*

3. *A general view of Atlantic blanket bog in the Owenduff, County Mayo. The large conspicuous hummocks are formed by the Silver-haired Moss. (Peter Foss).*

4. *A swallow hole in Atlantic blanket bog in County Mayo. The Royal Fern can be seen protruding at the mouth. (Peter Foss).*

5. *Pipewort growing around the edges of a lakes in Atlantic blanket bog. (Gerry Doyle)*

6. *An island in a lake in Atlantic blanket bog vegetation in the Owenduff, County Mayo. (Peter Foss)*

THE USES OF BOGS

Mary Tubridy and Catherine O'Connell

Nowadays, bogs like all wetlands are considered waste places and many people believe that they should be dug up, drained and changed into something dry and more "useful". In a country where peatland originally covered 17% of the land surface, man has learned to use bogs and peat in many different ways.

A Source of Fuel

The most common use of bogs as a source of fuel started a thousand years ago. By the 17th century, trees had almost disappeared from Ireland and turf was the only available fuel for the majority of people. The practice of hand cutting has declined in the last decade particularly in the Midlands with the possibility that this aspect of our peatland heritage may soon be lost.

The traditional method of cutting turf involved a team of three people; a cutter, a catcher and a wheeler. The cutter used a special type of spade called a "sléan", with a wing set at right angles to the blade. After a sod was cut, it was thrown to the catcher who stacked the wet sods on a flat open barrow. The wheeler brought them to a dry spreading ground where they were laid down to dry (Figure 5). The ways in which the sods were arranged to dry varied around the country. The turf was brought home and stored in stacks or ricks near the house. Hand turf-cutting, although rare in the Midlands is still widely practiced in the west of Ireland and involves two or more people. Competitions are held at many venues each year to discover the quickest and most efficient wielder of the sléan.

Figure 5—Turning sods of peat to dry in the west of Ireland. When dry, the sods are stacked in ricks as seen in the background. (Photograph courtesy of the Office of Public Works).

The advent of "Difco" peat cutting machines or "sausage" machines which can be attached to the back of a tractor means that for some people peat cutting is no longer a labour intensive chore. By means of an extractor which has a sharp blade, the wet peat is drawn up by the machine and exuded as a series of long "sausages" on the surface of the bog. This peat "sausage" is allowed to dry. As it does, it cracks at regular intervals forming sods, which are stacked in the same way as hand-cut peat.

Commercial methods of peat exploitation have been developed by Bord na Móna who are second only to their counterparts in Russia in the scale of their operations. Bord na Móna manufacture a range of peat products. These include sod peat and milled peat both of which can be burned to generate electricity. Milled peat is also compressed at high temperatures and made into peat briquettes, which are used as a domestic fuel. Bord na Móna moss peat is familiar to gardeners around the world, who use it as a source of organic material to enrich and improve the water-holding capacity of soils.

An Integral Part of Country Life
In the last century, bogs not only supplied fuel, but also provided many materials needed by a farming family. Sods cut from the bog could be used to roof a cottage and fossil timber dug out of the peat provided thick beams for rafters. The poor survived by farming bogland as this was given rent free by the landlord. Very often they built cabins from dried peat sods on the bog. The bog also supplied fertiliser and lime. The fertiliser was made by burning scraw (bog vegetation) and collecting the ash, while lime was dug out from the marl layer found under the peat in the Midlands. Farmers used bogs for rough grazing, a practice which became more important particularly after the appearance of large scale sheep farming in the west of Ireland. Due to the multiplicity of uses, it is not surprising that when farmers spoke of their bog it was always called the "best bog in Ireland".

Bogs also had more unusual uses. They were used as storehouses or fridges for perishable food, particularly butter. Turfcutters often come across wooden casks containing butter which were buried in the peat. The remarkable preserving powers of peat were used instead of salt to keep the butter fresh. This bog butter retains its colour and freshness for a few hundred years. In the course of time, however, the composition and flavour of the butter changes to resemble cream cheese.

The acid water in bog pools has been used by flax growers in a process known as retting. This process allowed the plants to decompose sufficiently to free the fibres which were later used to weave linen. Such retting pools are still to be seen around the margins of some bogs particularly in Northern Ireland.

Management for Game
Traditionally undisturbed raised and blanket bogs were managed by estate owners for game birds, particularly the Red Grouse. As part of this management programme alternate sections of the bog were burned on a ten year cycle. This produced a mosaic of Ling Heather of different ages necessary for the feeding and breeding habits of the Grouse. Today this tradition, although not as widespread as previously, is encouraged by Regional

Game Councils (RGCs). The overall decline in this activity is attributed to changing landuse patterns and the development of bogs for other purposes. This has resulted in the loss of suitable habitats for Grouse and a decline in the numbers of this bird nationally. Measures are currently being taken by the RGC to rectify this problem by managing a series of bogs for Grouse.

Red Grouse

E. WYMER

Uses of Bog Plants

In this century the antiseptic qualities of peat were recognised during the First World War. Tons of *Sphagnum* peat were used in the manufacture of wound dressings. Other bog plants supplied valuable extracts used in medicine; for example, an extract from Sundew was used as a treatment for warts.

Some bog plants have also been used in non-medicinal practices; for example, Cranberries have been used to make cranberry sauce and Ling Heather flowers have been used in wine making. The leaves of Bog Myrtle have been used as an alternative flavouring to hops in the fermentation of mead.

***Plate 6* Atlantic Blanket Bog**
1. *Atlantic Blanket Bog in Mayo showing the golden brown colour of this peatland in winter. (Peter Foss)*

2. *The yellow flowers of the Bog Asphodel are conspicuous on bogs in June and July. (Office of Public Works)*

3. *Milkwort is a typical species of Atlantic blanket bog vegetation. (Office of Public Works)*

4. *A section of visually disruptive forestry on Atlantic blanket bog in County Mayo. (Peter Foss)*

5. *Surface drain on Atlantic blanket bog in Mayo containing Brambles and other species not found on the open bog surface. (Peter Foss)*

6. *Atlantic blanket bog landscape in Connemara. (Caitríona Douglas).*

Artistic Work in Peat and Bog Wood

Many objects have been hand-crafted either from peat itself or from the wood (Pine or Oak) which lies within the bog. In the 19th century, in Killarney, hand carved ornaments and jewellery made from bog Oak, were sold to tourists. The jewellery included Tara broaches and celtic crosses, which were decorated with traditional shamrock and harp motifs. While much of the carving was coarse, some pieces were finely carved and occasionally mounted in gold, reputedly originating from Wicklow (Figure 6).

Figure 6—An Irish Harp carved from bog Oak and decorated with shamrocks.

(Photograph courtesy of Catherine O'Connell).

Peat was also used in the production of peat postcards. One such card posted in 1904 states: "This card is made from paper manufactured by Callender Paper Mills, Celbridge, from peat taken from the bog of Allen." The card is dark brown in colour and shows a colleen with an appropriate verse.

Today there are a number of companies manufacturing a range of souvenir items made from materials removed from peatlands. The Irish Bog Oak and Wood Company of Blessington produce clocks and lamps made from Pine and Oak timber removed from bogs. Another company, Owencraft of Ballyshannon produces a wide range of ornaments which are hand made from highly polished compressed peat. These include Celtic crosses and various statues associated with Irish country life and mythology.

The Oak, Yew and Pine that has been preserved in bogs for up to 4,000 years is a source of inspiration to Michael Casey of Barley Harbour, County Longford, a sculptor of bog wood. The knarled pieces of bog wood are transformed by the artist into free-form sculptures that capture the hidden beauty of the age old timber. After its removal from the bog, the wood is dried for two years before it is ready for sculpting and sanding. The final step before the emergence of the "bog-form" is polishing with bees wax.

THE ARCHAEOLOGY OF PEATLANDS

Ann Lynch, Seamas Caulfield & Barry Raftery

Information obtained by studying the material remains of man's past such as his tools, weapons, houses, and tombs allows us to reconstruct aspects of different cultures from prehistoric times right up to the recent past. A lot of information has been gained from the excavation of peatlands. This is because of the extraordinary state of preservation of a very wide range of objects found in peat. How does this come about?

The anaerobic conditions (the lack of oxygen) which prevail in peatlands mean that organic materials such as leather, wood, bone and textiles survive in excellent condition. The excavation of ancient settlements in peatlands can therefore tell us a lot about ancient societies. Techniques of building houses, barns, fences and carts can be deduced. The types of clothing which the people wore can often be reconstructed. Artistic work in wood or textiles can tell us something about the level of sophistication of the society in question. If we are lucky, we may even gain insights into their religious or ritual activities.

Many of the archaeological discoveries in peatlands are made by chance (usually during turf cutting) and perhaps the most dramatic of these are the bog burials. Throughout the ages, people have been buried in bogs. These people either met their deaths through strangulation, hanging or decapitation, after which their bodies were buried in a bog or they accidentally fell into bog holes and drowned. Many bog burials have been found in Britain and Denmark but some have also been recovered from Irish bogs, the most recent being from Meenybradden, County Donegal (Figure 7). When the peat cover has been carefully removed from these burials, the bodies have a remarkably life-like appearance. The skin usually has undergone a tanning process in the peat and has the appearance and texture of leather. The colour and type of hair can often still be seen. The clothing in which they were buried is still in place, usually woollen or hide cloaks. Advances in modern technology mean that an ever increasing amount of information can be gained from these burials, for example, analysis of stomach contents can tell us what the victim ate for his/her last meal. Bog burials certainly tell us far more than the skeletons removed from dryland sites!

Perhaps less dramatic, but equally important, are the thousands of objects found over the years in peatlands and now housed in the National Museum of Ireland. The types of objects found range from artefacts in gold or silver to bronze spearheads, amber beads, flint arrowheads, stone axeheads, leather shoes, wooden vessels, and bog butter. Most of the objects were probably lost by their owners as they travelled to and fro across the bogs. Traffic across the bogs must have been quite heavy considering the number of trackways (also known as Toghers) which have been found (Figure 8).

In addition to structures and objects found *in* the peat, we should not forget that many sites of archaeological interest lie *under* the peat, on the mineral soil. These sites are often only discovered when the peat cover has been fully removed as was the case at Boora, County Offaly where one of the earliest occupation sites in Ireland was revealed, dating to circa 7,000 BC. In some upland areas, where the blanket peat is not very deep, traces of ancient field systems which underlie the peat, can be seen.

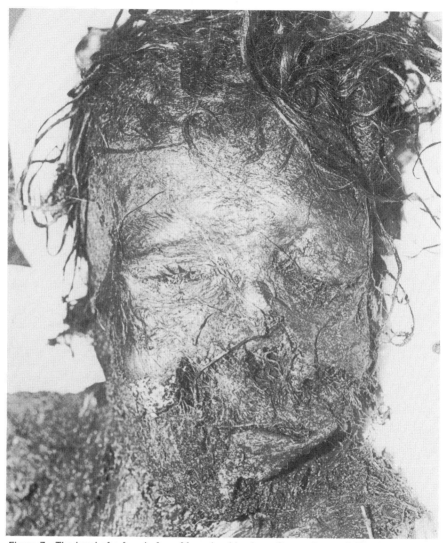

Figure 7—The head of a female from Meenybradden bog, County Donegal. This head dates to the late sixteenth century. (Photograph courtesy of the National Museum of Ireland).

Plate 7 Mountain Blanket Bog

1. Mountain blanket bog landscape at Liffey Head, County Wicklow. (Peter Foss)
2. Aquatic Bog Moss and the leaves and flowers of Bog Cotton in a bog pool. (Brian Madden)
3. Oak Eggar caterpillar feeding on Ling Heather. (Caitríona Douglas)
4. Peat cutting—the traditional way. (Office of Public Works)
5. A conspicuous plant on bogs in summer is the Cross-leaved Heath. (Office of Public Works)
6. The Clubmoss is a characteristic plant of Mountain blanket bog. (Peter Foss)

Figure 8—An oakwood trackway or Togher at Corlea, County Longford. The timbers were dated by dendrochronology to 148 BC. (Photograph courtesy of Barry Raftery).

In conclusion, peatlands are clearly a vital resource as far as our archaeological heritage is concerned. It is therefore important that wherever tracts of bog are being commercially developed, there should be some supervision by an archaeologist to ensure that any artefacts or structures uncovered are fully recorded and/or retrieved.

In the next two sections, Seamas Caulfield and Barry Raftery will describe some of the insights that have been gained from recent excavation of field systems and bog trackways respectively.

A Pre-bog Stone Age Farmland

Under the blanket bog in Mayo, at Behy/Glenulra, lies a field system which has not been grazed for the last 4,000 years. The layout of these fields, (Figure 9), is similar to those that are in use today in many parts of Ireland. The long parallel walls and the shorter cross walls divide up the landscape into fields, some of which contain enclosures and tombs. The blanket bog grew up to engulf them so that today they lie covered by peat to a depth of four metres. The site was discovered only when the bog was partly cut away for fuel. A megalithic tomb was revealed and the lines of stone walls were mapped to give the plan presented.

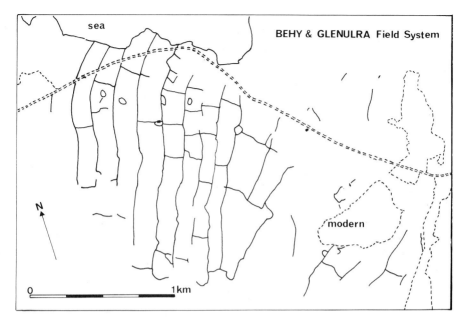

Figure 9—Pre-bog Field System at Behy/Glenulra, County Mayo. This field system was constructed circa 4,000 years ago. The solid lines represent the 4,000 year walls of the field system and the dotted lines indicate the walls of modern fields dated at 1838 AD. (Photograph courtesy of Seamas Caulfield).

Initially only that part of the site where the bog was being cut could be mapped, but the walls which disappear under the uncut bog have been traced in recent years. These walls survive in places up to one metre high above the old ground surface. Even in deep bogs, the walls can be traced using long iron probes which can be easily pushed into the bog until they hit the mineral soil or solid structure beneath. By probing at right angles across the line of a wall, it is not too difficult to establish the level of the old ground surface under the bog and the position and height of the wall built on the surface (Figure 10).

The Behy/Glenulra fields allow us to reach a number of conclusions about the prehistoric people who built them and about the conditions under which they farmed the land.

1. The Pine forest had been virtually completely removed from this extensive area otherwise it would have been impossible to retain the parallel system of wall layout.

2. The walls were laid out in an organised pattern and total over 30 km in length. Therefore there must have been a sizable community acting to an agreed or imposed plan.

3. The total area enclosed by the fields of 400 ha indicates that these fields were used for pasture.

45

Figure 10—A stone age wall being discovered under blanket bog in Mayo. By inserting a 4 m probe (seen on the right hand side) into the bog, the depth of peat above the mineral soil and the position of walls marking ancient field boundaries (indicated by the bamboo canes in the centre of the photograph) can be determined. (Photograph courtesy of Seamas Caulfield).

4. Growing conditions must have been better then because the horizontal parallel strips of fields extend over the top of the hill at an altitude close to 250 m. Modern fields in west Mayo do not extend to this altitude.

Many questions still remain to be answered. Was the decision to lay out the fields taken by a ruling chieftain or was it made more democratically by a "village council" such as a group of village elders? Does the division of the landscape into separate strips, subdivided into fields indicate private property and independent farmers at this early stage or were the fields designed for the easy management of herds and pasture in a system of communal farming?

Plate 8 Mountain Blanket Bog
1. *Surface drain in mountain blanket bog at Liffey Head, County Wicklow. (Peter Foss)*
2. *Bog Cotton is a species typical of the wetter areas on bogs. (Caitriona Douglas)*
3. *A variety of lichens colonising an area of bare peat. The red topped matchstick Lichen is conspicuous. (Peter Foss)*
4. *Mountain blanket bog and lakes in winter at Liffey Head, County Wicklow. (Peter Foss)*
5. *Mountain peat erosion on Minaun Heights, Achill, County Mayo. (Peter Foss)*
6. *Ling Heather flowers in August and September on bogs. (Peter Foss)*

The importance of discovering and studying field systems under the blanket bog is that it throws a new light on the stage of development of prehistoric agriculture. The radiocarbon dates for the Behy/Glenulra site indicate that the fields were constructed more than 5,000 years ago and that the bog had begun to grow and engulf the fields within a 1,000 years. These dates suggest that the Irish field systems pre-date similar field systems found elsewhere in Europe, by 1000 years. It is highly unlikely that Neolithic (Stone Age) fields were only in use in those areas where they are preserved today by the blanket bog. Behy/Glenulra therefore provides a real model as to what the farming conditions would have been like, and how the entire landscape may have been organised around places like Newgrange or Stonehenge. These places may not have had exactly similar field systems but we know from the pre-bog fields that extensive developed field systems were well established by the time many of the spectacular ritual monuments were constructed.

Trackways in Corlea Bog, County Longford

In the past vast tracts of intact raised bog would have provided serious obstacles to travel at most times of the year, and would have been virtually impassable in winter. From at least the Bronze Age onwards, the inhabitants surrounding raised bogs constructed elaborate trackways or Toghers across the soggy bogland to facilitate movement both by pedestrians and wheeled vehicles. These toghers were particularly common in Counties Offaly, Meath, Westmeath, Leitrim, Longford, Kildare, Tipperary and Galway.

Recent excavations in Corlea bog, County Longford have revealed some interesting facts about the nature of prehistoric trackways in Ireland. Here, five tracks were built across the bog at different times. The most spectacular was a massive construction, composed of planks of Oak, each up to 3.5 m long, which rested on parallel pairs of long runners, at right angles to the direction of the trackway (Figure 8). In places the Oak planks were secured by sharpened pegs of Birch driven through mortices at their ends. This great road—for such it may be described—extended for a distance of almost 1 km across the bog. Thanks to dendrochronology (the study of tree rings), it has been established that the trees used for it were felled in 148 BC.

There were also three less substantial tracks of brushwood at Corlea. Two of these were composed of tightly-packed, Birch branches lying parallel to the direction of the track. These provided a thick, spongy walking surface. The third track was partly made of Birch branches laid down in a similar manner but also incorporated woven hurdles in its construction. These had been made separately in an upright position before being transported to the site and laid end-to-end like mats across the bog. One of these tracks has been dated by radiocarbon determination to 1020 BC.

The final track at Corlea was simply made by laying narrow Oak planks end-to-end on short, transverse sleepers. This track has been dated to 587 AD.

These trackways give us some ideas about the locations of local population centres around raised bogs in the past. They were probably constructed to enable groups of people to remain in contact with one another. The Oak trackway at Corlea was capable of carrying wheeled vehicles. The analysis of the structure of each of the different trackways on the bog throws light on the sophistication of construction techniques at the time and the types of raw materials that were available in the area for such work.

VEGETATION HISTORY

Catherine O'Connell

Each year pollen produced by the vegetation growing on the bog surface and the vegetation of the surrounding landscape is trapped in the upper peat layer of the bog. In fact there is so much pollen trapped in the peat of a bog that the poet Seamus Heaney's description of them as "pollen bins" is very appropriate. These huge quantities of pollen grains can only be seen with the help of a microscope. Counting the different types of pollen grains in a sample of peat gives an idea of the vegetation present in the landscape of Ireland at a given time in the past. So by looking at the pollen content of successive samples down through the peat profile, it is just like turning the pages of a history book. You can record and see the changes in the vegetation history of an area. In this way the history of the vegetation of Ireland has been reconstructed since the last Ice Age.

About 10,000 years ago Ireland was coming out of the grips of an ice age. The types of pollen found in the lake muds beneath the peat mass shows that the country was covered with tundra vegetation, composed of low growing cushion plants and hardy shrubs, similar to that found in northern Canada and Iceland today. As the climate warmed up the ice melted. This allowed temperate, relatively frost sensitive trees to return to Ireland from the continent, by migrating over the land connections that existed between Ireland, Britain and Europe. Birch was the first tree to colonise the barren expanse of Ireland, followed by Pine and Hazel. By 7,000 years ago the woodlands of Ireland had become established, with Elm, Oak, Alder and Hazel growing on the fertile soils and Pine and Birch on poorer soils. At this time it is possible to imagine most of the country covered by woodland, interrupted by shallow lakes, which were becoming infilled with Reed and fen communities. By 7,000 years ago this infilling process of the lakes in the Midlands, caused by the accumulation of dead plant remains was complete and the Bog Moss *(Sphagnum)* became abundant on the surface of the bog. The arrival of this moss marks the beginning of acid peat formation and the start of raised bog development. In western Ireland, blanket peat development had also started by this time in low lying depressions in the landscape.

From 7,000 to 5,000 years ago "silence" reigned in the woodlands until the slash and crack of the first farmers, the Neolithic or Stone Age farmers was heard. These people cleared Elm and Hazel from the good soils to make room for their animals and to grow crops. This clearance of woodland may be associated with the sudden decline in the pollen of Elm, known in scientific circles as the "Elm decline" (Figure 11) and the appearance of the pollen of weeds such as Plantain, Dandelion and Dock. Similarly these farmers also cleared the Pinewoods on the poorer soils in the west of Ireland using stone axes to fell the trees which were then burned along with the underbrush to create agricultural land.

The clearance of Irish woodlands for agriculture initiated by Stone Age farmers continued for a further 5,000 years and resulted in the relatively treeless landscape familiar to us

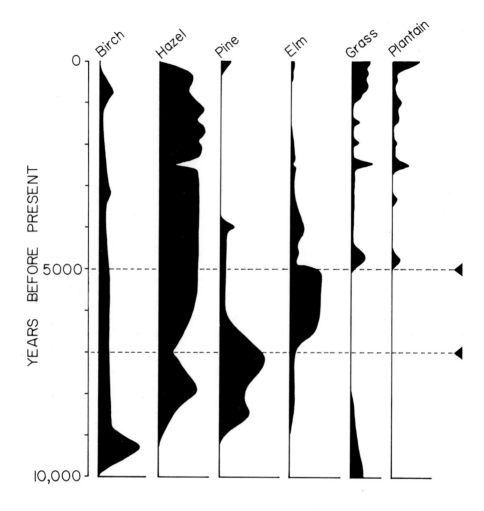

Figure 11—A generalised pollen diagram for the last 10,000 years. Only six species curves are presented. These are Birch, Pine, Hazel, Elm, Grass and Plantain. The pollen diagram is divided into three zones. During the first zone from 10,000 to 7,000 years ago trees such as Birch, Pine and Hazel invaded the country. The second zone from 7,000 to 5,000, is the woodland phase marked by large amounts of Elm pollen. The final phase is from 5,000 to the present day beginning with the "Elm decline" and characterised by increases in pollen of grass and Plantain, indicative of farming activities. This zone ends with the reintroduction of species like Pine 300 years ago.

today. In the pollen records, this gradual reduction in trees is associated with the continuous presence of grass, cereal and weed pollen such as Plantain and Dandelion (Figure 12). In peat samples close to the surface of the bog it is possible to detect the pollen of exotic species including conifers, Beech and Lime, trees introduced to Ireland from abroad during the Tudor plantations of the late 16th century.

Figure 12—A pollen grain of a weed species, the Dandelion magnified 2,000 times.

(Photograph courtesy of Peter Foss).

The unearthing of the mysterious history preserved in our peatlands, tell us of a past unrecorded in history books. If bogs are allowed to continue their growth, the future impacts of man on the environment will also be preserved in the living peaty pages o' this unique history book.

PEATLAND EXPLOITATION IN THE REPUBLIC OF IRELAND

John Cross

Centuries of exploitation have taken their toll on the peatlands of Ireland. The rate of exploitation has increased dramatically in the last ten years, so much so that steps to conserve some of the best examples of the different peatland types will have to be taken without delay. In the next two chapters we will examine the rates of, and reasons for the disappearance of raised and blanket bogs.

Raised Bogs

Raised bogs once covered 311,000 ha of the Republic of Ireland. In 1974, 65,000 ha of the original area remained relatively undisturbed or intact. Eleven years later in 1985, conservationists were shocked when survey work conducted by the Forest & Wildlife Service (FWS) revealed that only 20,000 ha of this area remained intact, about one fifteenth of the original area! An example will illustrate this point. In 1974 the eight counties of Galway, Kildare, Laois, Louth, Meath, Offaly, Roscommon and North Tipperary, had 39,000 ha of intact raised bog. In 1985 there was only 11,000 ha remaining with nature reserve potential. However, all of the sites identified were damaged to some degree by marginal drainage, frequent fires and turf cutting. Two of the counties, Louth and Meath, had no peatlands left and three others, Kildare, Laois and Roscommon have very few sites remaining. Taking the Republic as a whole less than 5% of the raised bogs remain with nature reserve potential (Figure 13).

The main cause for the decline of raised bogs was found to be peat cutting. Of the original area of raised bog 92% has been classified as cutaway bog. Private cutting by hand has contributed most to the loss of intact bog, which is not surprising for it has been going on for centuries. Bord na Móna, the Irish Peat Development Authority has cut away just under a quarter of the raised bogs, but all of that has occurred in the last forty years, illustrating the importance of and the threat posed by, mechanisation. The recently developed "Difco" machines (or "sausage" peat machines) which can be attached to tractors are a serious new threat to the remaining intact raised bogs (Figure 14). The use of these machines has increased since it became possible for private individuals to obtain grants for peat extraction under the Turf Development Act, 1981. One of the major problems posed by private peat cutting is that it nibbles away at every bog so that there is no bog that is entirely free from some degree of damage. Drainage, especially arterial drainage is another indirect threat to bogs. These schemes have resulted in a general lowering of the water levels over a wide area and some of the raised bogs may be drying out as a result.

Blanket Bogs

Blanket bog once covered 772,000 ha of the Republic of Ireland, well over twice the area of raised bog. These bogs are under considerable threat from a combination of peat cutting and afforestation. Forests have been planted on about 18% of the blanket bogs and it is estimated that a further 15% are affected by peat cutting. This still leaves over half a million hectares but out of this, large areas are damaged by over-grazing and repeated burning. Afforestation and peat cutting activities by private individuals

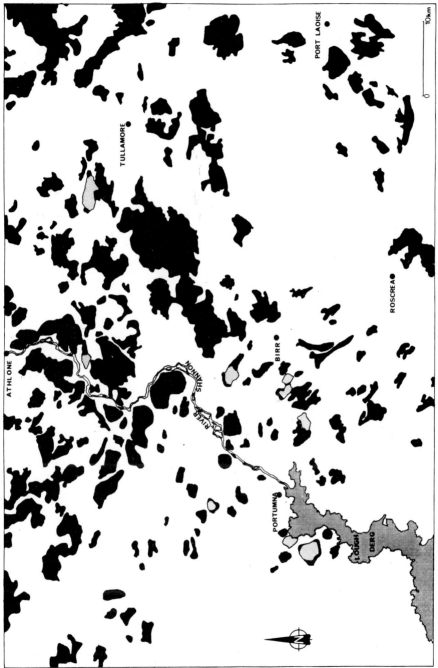

Figure 13—A map of the central Midlands showing the original area of raised bogs. The shaded areas represent peatlands of no conservation value while the grey areas represent potential nature reserves.

and Bord na Móna are fragmenting many important blanket bog areas, such as south Connemara in County Galway. The overall result of these activities is that extensive tracts of undamaged blanket bog with nature reserve potential are becoming rare (Figure 14).

Rates of Extinction of Raised and Blanket Bogs

Over 3,000 ha of raised bogs are being cut away each year. At this rate all the bogs of scientific interest, the potential nature reserves, east of the river Shannon will have disappeared by 1993 and those west of the Shannon by 1997 at the latest. Blanket bogs are disappearing more slowly—at present rates of decline they may last another one hundred years—but the most important areas could well go long before that.

In view of this a systematic county by county survey of bogs is being conducted throughout the country, by the FWS in order to identify potential nature reserves. The next step is to ensure that the potential nature reserves identified to date are conserved as National Nature Reserves. In the meantime the bodies responsible for peatland exploitation have been informed of the location of these sites. Unless we act now to conserve these bogs further damage to them may mean that expensive remedial measures will be required at a future date to safeguard them.

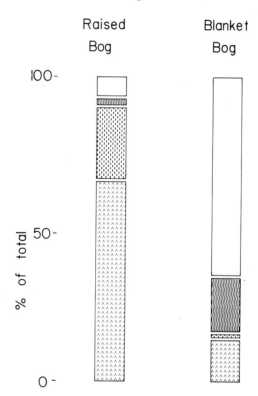

Figure 14—Losses of raised and blanket bogs up to 1985. The peak symbol represents areas lost through private peat cutting, the dashed symbol represents the area cut by Bord na Móna, the waved lines represent afforested peatlands and the white area represents intact peatland.

PEATLAND EXPLOITATION IN NORTHERN IRELAND

David Dunlop

At one time peatland covered much of Northern Ireland but this resource has been much reduced over the past few centuries by peat cutting for fuel and draining for agriculture. A survey carried out in 1956 estimated that 17.8% (264,000 ha) of Northern Ireland was covered by peatlands. Another survey in 1979 put the figure at 12.4% (171,265 ha). Three-quarters of this area (130,000 ha) was mountain blanket bog and most of the rest was raised bog. At this time very little fen was left in Northern Ireland. In 1979, about half of the remaining peatland area was intact while the other half had been irreversibly damaged through human activity. Since the introduction of the "Difco" or "sausage" peat machines in the 1980's the area of intact bog has decreased rapidly, though we cannot say precisely how much peatland has been affected as yet.

In 1985, The Wildlife Order (NI) was passed giving our Department of the Environment's Countryside and Wildlife Branch greater powers to conserve wildlife and wildlife habitats. Because the threat to peatlands was so serious a survey of raised bogs was given priority and important peatland sites were identified. The Countryside and Wildlife Branch is currently negotiating with the owners of these sites to ensure that they are conserved as National Nature Reserves or areas of special scientific interest.

Large areas of the hills in Northern Ireland are covered in mountain blanket bog. These areas should also be surveyed to identify important sites. It is a race against time as blanket bogs continue to be damaged by the new peat extraction methods. The blanket bog on and around Slieveanorra, a hill on the northern part of the Antrim Plateau, provides an example of the problem. When it was surveyed in 1979 it was found to be intact but in the 1980's large areas had been irreversibly damaged by mechanised peat cutting.

In Northern Ireland there is no large, semi-state body like Bord na Móna involved in the business of commercial peat extraction. However, Government grants are available from the Local Enterprise Development Unit (LEDU) to help people set up small peat extraction businesses. This has helped to promote widespread use of the Difco machines. LEDU have been advised by the DoE Countryside and Wildlife Branch about the importance of not damaging valuable peatlands. Co-operation between these two bodies and the DoE Town and Country Planning Service should prevent public money being used to subsidise the destruction of our remaining good peatland sites.

EROSION OF MOUNTAIN BLANKET BOGS

Richard Bradshaw

Mountain blanket bogs are not the undamaged blankets of peat we envisage. Quite often they are broken up by deep gullies and cracks. When these cracks are subjected to erosion, peat is washed away until all that is left are dried chunks of intact peat called "haggs". With every storm, erosion removes small amounts of peat at the edge of the bare haggs and in dry periods the peat blows away with the wind. As a result of this erosion by wind and water the surviving haggs point downslope and downwind. You can find damaged and eroding blanket bog in every mountain range in the country. Only the Slieve Blooms in Counties Laois and Offaly have large areas of relatively undamaged mountain blanket bog.

Why are our mountain blanket bogs eroding in this way? A number of explanations have been suggested.

The first cause may be the disturbance caused by human activity and farming practices. Human damage of mountain blanket bogs includes turf cutting, both mechanical and hand cutting, afforestation, motor-bike scrambling, regular burning and more indirectly the effect of air pollution especially along the east coast. For centuries mountain blanket bogs have been used for sheep grazing which causes compaction of the peat from trampling and may lead to the removal of the stabilising vegetation cover through over-grazing.

The second cause of mountain blanket bog erosion could be that it is a natural process or a response to climatic change. It is a process that has been going on for some time as eroded peat has been washing into Arts Lough in the Wicklow Mountains for over 3,000 years. Mountain blanket bogs are sensitive to changes in rainfall, temperature and wind speed. An increase in rainfall coupled with more severe winters could damage the most exposed peatlands, increasing the extent of erosion.

The most dramatic form of peat erosion is a "bog burst" or peat flow. Sections of peat on sloped areas can break off from the main body of a blanket bog and flow downslope pushing over trees and destroying houses in much the same way as a volcanic lava flow destroys everything in its path. These bog bursts usually happen after heavy rain in the autumn. It is thought that the living plant skin of the bog tears due to stress and the unstable liquid centre flows under the influence of gravity. Bog flows can lead to further erosion if the damage is not quickly healed by plant growth.

To date there is no simple explanation for blanket bog erosion. It seems likely that erosion is a result of a combination of several different factors. While man has contributed to the damage, he may not be entirely to blame as some erosion of mountain blanket bog is probably quite natural.

MANAGEMENT OF CONSERVED PEATLANDS

Mary Tubridy

An undisturbed peatland requires little management other than warding off potential threats such as fire. However, there are no totally undisturbed bogs in Ireland: all bogs, even the best ones have been damaged to some degree. This means that any bog acquired for conservation requires management in order to repair the damage. Apart from curative measures, an active management strategy is needed to control threats such as burning and dumping and to accommodate visitors to the bog. In this way proper management can actually increase the scientific and recreational value of a conserved bog.

Management Plan

Accepting that management is necessary, how is it planned? After acquisition it is necessary to prepare a comprehensive report which contains information on the scientific value of the bog including the vegetation, fauna and history. An assessment of how the site has been damaged in the past and of future threats is also necessary as well as information on the tourist potential of the site including estimates of the number of visitors and the likely impact on the local community. This information may already be available but more often it is necessary to carry out field studies and research. From the results of this research a management plan is prepared, which sets out the aims of management as well as the means of carrying out the work, the time taken and the expense involved.

This is the first step in management. A management plan may take months to research and compile but will only apply for a limited period as management experience will lead to a re-assessment of priorities, or features of the site may change requiring different management practices.

The aims of management are:

1. To keep the bog as wet as possible.

2. To prevent fires and turf cutting.

3. To make the local community aware of the value of the bog.

4. To control the activities of visitors and researchers.

5. To keep up-to-date records of events on the bog and data collected.

6. To ensure recognition for the site by the Government as a National Nature Reserve if it is owned by a non-governmental organisation.

The most important factor which underlies all peatland management is the maintenance of a high water table in order to keep the bog wet. Once a bog has been damaged, the water table is lowered. To raise it again the drains on and around the bog must be blocked. The problem is accentuated by the establishment of trees such as Birch in the cutaway area surrounding the bog. The trees lower the water table by absorbing the water they need from the peat and therefore they must be removed. It may also be necessary to negotiate with neighbouring farmers to persuade them not to dig drains on the farmland adjacent to the bog which might affect the bog water table. Experiments should be set up which allow the wetness of the bog to be monitored and thereby calculate the effectiveness of drain blocking.

Fires can be prevented by controlling turf cutting and dumping. This means that people with turbary rights must be compensated or given alternative sites where they can cut turf. It is necessary to patrol the bog regularly in order to ensure that turf cutting does not occur and to watch for the threat of fires spreading from the surrounding land. If a fire does occur a plan must be operated to bring it under control as soon as possible as it could quickly destroy large areas of the bog.

Both of these aspects of the management plan illustrate the importance of making the local community aware of the value of the bog in their locality. The conservation and management of bogs can only succeed if people understand what is at stake and care enough to give their support and co-operation.

A conserved bog will attract visitors who must be carefully supervised so that their activities do not conflict with conservation. A wet bog surface is very susceptible to damage from trampling. It has been found that a single footprint on a bog can be seen two years later. This means that paths and boardwalks will have to be erected to direct visitors and car parks need to be made available. Educational material and information should be prepared and presented in an interpretation centre or by means of a permanent poster board or leaflets. Ideally guides should be employed during peak visitor periods to answer questions.

Manpower and Resources
The management plan should be implemented by a permanently employed site warden, a person who is based near the bog and who understands its value for conservation. The warden will need the help of conservation volunteers and casual labourers to fill in drains and build fences or paths as well as guides at peak visiting times. A bog should also have a "watcher", someone whose house overlooks the bog who could report on events occurring outside working hours. Volunteers will work free but resources will have to be found to cover the salary of the warden and pay other expenses.

This means that conservation of a bog costs more than the amount needed to purchase the bog in the first place. Regular finance will be needed each year to cover the costs of managing the bog. Some of this funding could be raised through sales of literature and other attractions could be developed nearby which might encourage more spending by visitors. If the bog is not cared for, illegal turf cutting, rubbish dumping or accidental fires will result in exploitation and not conservation of the bog. A management plan incorporating the various factors outlined above has been written for Mongan bog, County Offaly, a raised bog of international importance. This management plan is currently being implemented by An Taisce.

PEATLAND CONSERVATION AND THE LAW

Catherine O'Connell

Ireland's commitment to conservation is set out in the Wildlife Act 1976 and the Forest and Wildlife Service (FWS) are the Government body responsible for implementing this Act. The Wildlife Advisory Council (WAC) was established under the Wildlife Act and its function is to advise the Minister responsible for conservation in relation to policy, objectives and programmes of wildlife conservation.

Under the Wildlife Act there is legislation to protect animals and plants. The Flora Protection Order (1987), protects fifty-two named, rare, threatened and endangered plants. This means that it is an offence to pick, cut, uproot or collect specimens, or destroy or interfere with their habitats. A list (Red Data List) of rare and endangered plants has been compiled by the FWS and a number of the plants included in it are found in peatlands. The protection given to peatlands that are the habitats of a rare and threatened plant is such that they cannot be interfered with in any way without a licence from the FWS.

One of the important functions of the FWS has been the identification of peatland sites with potential nature reserve status. These peatlands are assessed and rated as being of international, national, regional or local importance. The rating of these peatlands by the FWS does not in itself offer any protection to them. For example, Clara bog County Offaly was drained in 1983 despite being rated as a site of international scientific importance. At present it is only the state-owned peatlands that are fully protected. So far, the Government has only established very few state-owned reserves, either NNRs or National Parks. Most of these were either already in state ownership being bought originally for forestry or for amenity use (National Parks). Funds for protecting scientifically important peatlands have been very limited indeed, and have only been made available for a few sites after considerable public pressure, for example, Pollardstown Fen and Clara bog. To date this is the only protective strategy that has been explored under the Wildlife Act in relation to peatlands. The difficulty with this strategy is that the Government seems unprepared to seriously finance the establishment of a network of peatland nature reserves necessary to conserve a representative sample of the variation and diversity of this ecosystem in Ireland.

The Wildlife Act lists a number of other ways in which scientifically important peatlands might be protected. The first of these is by arranging land use management agreements with (private) landowners. These could be useful in the agricultural areas found surrounding NNRs, for example, at Pollardstown fen any change in land use in the catchment, which includes the Curragh (4 km to the south-west) could adversely affect the supply of water to the fen in spite of the fact that the fen itself is a NNR. A management agreement for this area should encourage the maintenance of traditional land use by providing suitable financial assistance if necessary. This financial backing by the Government is the major obstacle to this particular strategy, as the Government is reluctant to compensate farmers. Such compensation would doubtless stimulate an interest in positive attitudes towards conservation in the farming community.

Alternatively the Government could support Non-Governmental Organisations (NGOs) by recognising their efforts to purchase and establish their own peatland nature reserves. These sites, once purchased, should then be recognised by the State as NNRs.

There are indirect ways in which the FWS can "protect" peatlands which would halt the exploitation of potential nature reserves. They can ensure that Government or EEC funds are not used to develop these sites. This can be done by screening various grant applications to check for possible conflicts with peatland conservation, including grant applications under the Turf Development Act 1981, the purchase of areas for afforestation, and EEC development grant applications.

Apart from the Wildlife Act, Ireland has accepted a range of responsibilities for wildlife conservation at an international level. To this end the Government has signed a number of international conventions and as a member of the EEC is subject to EEC legislation. These conventions impose restraints on the freedom of action by ratifying States. If broken they can lead to international embarrassment or legal action against the offending country by the European Commission. The International Conventions and EEC legislation which are of most relevance to peatlands are listed below.

1. EEC Directive on the Conservation of Wild Birds
This was adopted on 2 April 1979 and came into force in the Member States in April 1981. It provides for the protection and management of European wild birds and their eggs, nests and habitats. In Annex 1 of the EEC Directive three of the species listed are inhabitants of peatlands. These are the Golden Plover, the Merlin and the Greenland White-fronted Goose. Article 4 of the Directive requires every National Government to protect the habitats of Annex 1 species. This should be done by designating those peatlands inhabited by Annex 1 birds as Special Protection Areas (SPAs). This does not require purchase of the site. In Ireland thirty-five blanket bogs and five raised bogs have been identified that are used as roosting and feeding sites by Greenland White-fronted Geese. Two of these are National Nature Reserves, and a further three are scheduled to become NNRs. If all of these sites were designated as SPAs interference or development of them could be prevented at an international level. Should the Government refuse or fail to comply with this regulation they would have to face possible legal action in the European Court. This has happened at Duich Moss on Islay in Scotland where the European Commission have intervened in a legal case against the British Government.

In designating a peatland an SPA, the Government must make provision for the socio-economic implications of such a decision. This might involve financial compensation to the owner of the site which could prove to be a problem in Ireland under present Governmental policy. In view of this it seems likely that only those peatlands which are NNRs will be designated as SPAs under the EEC Directive.

2. EEC Regulation on Action by the Community relating to the Environment (ACE)
This regulation provides for community aid of up to 50% of the cost of projects aimed at the maintenance or re-establishment of seriously threatened biotopes which are of importance to the community in the context of the Bird Directive. There will be a new ACE Regulation later this year, with improved conditions for funding which might allow the purchase of threatened Annex 1 species' habitats (for example peatlands in the case of Greenland White-fronted Geese). This financial assistance will be available to National Governments unable to raise all of the necessary funding to protect these habitats.

3. Berne Convention on the Conservation of European Wildlife and Natural Habitats

This Convention was signed by Ireland in September 1979 and ratified on 23 April 1982. It provides for the protection of specified fauna, flora and their habitats threatened or endangered in Europe as a whole. There are no Irish peatland species listed under the Berne Convention. There are however three bog species listed under the Flora Protection Order which are endangered in Europe as a whole. Apart from protection for individual species, the Convention could apply to, and therefore protect peatlands by virtue of the fact that these habitats are threatened in Europe as a whole.

4. Bonn Convention on the Conservation of Migratory Species of Wild Animals

This was signed in Ireland in June 1980 and ratified on the 5 August 1983. It provides protection for species which migrate between different States, particularly endangered species. The Convention is fully implemented under the Wildlife Act. Its relevance to peatlands is in connection with the Greenland White-fronted Goose and the Golden Plover.

5. Ramsar Convention on Wetlands of International Importance especially as Waterfowl Habitats

This was signed by Ireland in 1975 and ratified on 15 November 1984. This convention relates to all wetland sites including peatlands. The Wexford Wildfowl Reserve at the North Slob in County Wexford was the first Irish site to be designated under the Convention. More recently three peatlands have been designated as Ramsar sites because of their wildfowl populations and their botanical importance. These bogs are protected under this convention. Apart from being bound by the convention to protect designated sites, the Government has agreed to "wise-use" of all national wetlands.

Since peatlands are a threatened European habitat, Ireland has an international obligation to establish a series of NNRs containing peatlands. This fact has been recognised by the European Parliament in their Resolution on the Protection of Irish Bogs (1983) and by the International Mires Conservation Group (1986). The National and International legislation exists to protect peatlands. It is therefore the reluctance of the Government to seriously finance a conservation programme or to seek financial aid for such a programme which is the single biggest stumbling block in Irish peatland conservation today. It is to be hoped that in the future the Government will realise its national and international obligations to conservation and establish a peatland acquisition fund and thereby avail of the special funding provided towards this end by the EEC.

CONSERVATION ORGANISATIONS

Neil Lockhart

There are a number of organisations concerned with conservation in Ireland at present. The most comprehensive list available is the *Directory of Organisations with Environmental Interests*, published jointly by An Taisce and the National Board for Science and Technology. In the present article the activities of those most directly concerned with peatland conservation are outlined. Contact addresses for those organisations listed may be found in the chapter entitled Sources of Further Information.

Conservation organisations can be divided into two groups; State or State-sponsored bodies and non-governmental organisations (NGOs). The most important State body is the Forest and Wildlife Service (FWS). The FWS is charged with overall responsibility for nature conservation in the Republic of Ireland under the Wildlife Act 1976. They conduct inventory surveys with a view to establishing a network of National Nature Reserves (NNRs). They also have responsibility for administering and implementing international laws and conventions. At present there are 38 NNRs in Ireland, seven of which are peatlands. The Conservation Section of FWS produces posters and occasional pamphlets dealing with conservation matters. (The FWS has recently been divided into the Forestry Service and the Wildlife Service).

The other State body with an important role in peatland conservation is the National Parks and Monuments Service of the Office of Public Works (OPW). They administer three National Parks; Killarney, County Kerry; Glenveagh, County Donegal and Connemara, County Galway. These contain important blanket bogs. The OPW also produce information leaflets as part of their interpretive facilities for visitors to these areas.

An Foras Forbartha (AFF) is a State-sponsored Institute which undertakes research into matters concerning physical planning and development in Ireland. It produces numerous reports on environmental issues and has published the important inventory *Areas of Scientific Interest in Ireland* which lists and describes many of the most valuable Irish peatland sites.

Of the non-governmental organisations (NGOs), the largest and best known is An Taisce. Established in 1948 and with a membership of around 6,000, An Taisce's conservation interests are diverse. Their Wildlife Committee has actively campaigned for peatland conservation for a number of years. As a result An Taisce now owns 1,065 ha of blanket bog at Crocknafarragh, County Donegal, an important fen at Bellacorick, County Mayo and is currently negotiating the transfer of the internationally important raised bog at Mongan, County Offaly from Bord na Móna. Occasionally articles on peatlands are published in An Taisce's quarterly journal *Living Heritage*.

The Irish Wildlife Federation (IWF) is a more recently established NGO, with about 2,000 members and nine regional branches. They campaign actively for peatland conservation and have organised work-camps for volunteers, through their Ground-work program, to fill in drains on Mongan bog and Clara bog in County Offaly. Articles and news items on peatlands frequently appear in their quarterly newsletter *The Badger*.

The Irish Wildbird Conservancy (IWC) also have an interest in peatland conservation as peatlands are an important habitat for many species of bird. With about 4,000 members the IWC is a powerful lobby for conservation and has organised conferences on peatlands and published articles on bogs in its quarterly newsletter *IWC News* and its journal *Irish Birds*.

The Irish Peatland Conservation Council (IPCC) is an NGO set up in 1982. It aims to promote peatland conservation. It produces educational material, lobbies government and raises funds to purchase threatened peatland sites through the "Save the Bogs Campaign". It works in close co-operation with a similar NGO established in the Netherlands in 1983 called the Dutch Foundation for the Conservation of Irish Bogs.

The Dutch Foundation have successfully raised funds to buy Scragh Bog, County Westmeath and have received donations from the Dutch World Wildlife Fund which the IPCC is using to purchase several others. The ownership of these bogs will be transfered to the Irish Government and they will be managed as NNRs or National Parks. The Dutch Foundation produce a range of educational materials about peatlands.

In Northern Ireland there are two Government bodies concerned with peatland conservation. The first of these is the Countryside and Wildlife Branch of the Department of the Environment (DoE). The aims of the Branch are to protect the best natural, unspoilt and scenic areas of the country. In this capacity they have designated five peatland sites as NNRs and are negotiating with the owners of other important sites. These represent the best national examples of this habitat type in Northern Ireland. They provide Country Parks which are designed to promote an understanding of the countryside among the public. One of the Country Parks contains peatland. Further information and leaflets about these sites is available from the DoE Countryside and Wildlife Branch.

The second Government body concerned with peatland conservation in Northern Ireland is the Forest Service of the Department of Agriculture (DoA). This body owns and manages a number of Forest Nature Reserves, thirteen of which contain peatland. Further information is available from the DoA.

The Ulster Trust for Nature Conservation (UTNC) is an NGO with about 900 members which manages a network of fourteen Nature Reserves, two of which contain peatland. News items and articles on peatlands have appeared in the journal of the UTNC, *The Irish Hare*, published three times a year.

STUDENT INVESTIGATIONS OF A PEATLAND ECOSYSTEM

Edwin Wymer

The previous chapters have given you a wide range of information about bogs. The next thing you will want to do is to organise a group visit to a bog. There may be one locally or you can choose one from the chapters on Places to Visit. You will find your visit more rewarding if your group carries out its own study of the area as there is no better way to learn about bogs than by first hand experience.

Before you set off there are a few important points to take note of:

Bogs are wet places and can be dangerous. Never visit a bog on your own. Make sure you bring a waterproof coat, trousers and wellington boots. When you are walking on the bog, watch out for bright green areas which may hide pools or bog holes left by turf cutters. Approach bog pools with extreme caution as the ground surrounding them may be nothing more than an unstable raft of vegetation. Bring along a half inch or one inch ordnance survey map to help you get your bearings. Leave at least half a day free to work on the bog and if working in the afternoon bring a torch just in case. Never work on your own.

Some of you may not be too familiar with terms like ecology, ecosystems or nutrient cycling. You have probably heard the term *ecology* before. What does it mean? It is a study of the interrelationships of living organisms and their physical environment. This interaction is constantly occurring. In fact you are taking part in it yourself at this moment. An ecosystem is simply a place where plants and animals (living organisms) and the non-living environment interact to form a natural system. Bogs and fens are both examples of ecosystems. Both have plants and animals and a physical environment (for example peat, air and water).

Nutrient cycling is a fundamental ecological process that is continually occurring in all ecosystems. Where do the plants get their raw materials for life? In order to survive, plants and animals must obtain nutrients such as carbon, nitrogen and phosphorus. Most plants obtain their nutrients from the atmosphere, from the soil (peat in the case of a bog) and also from rainwater. The animals get their nutrients from eating plants or other animals. In every ecosystem dead plants and animals and their waste products are decomposed (broken down) by another important group of organisms, the decomposers. Thus the nutrients are released into the environment for uptake by the plants. Bacteria and fungi are common decomposers. They complete the recycling of nutrients. The efficiency of recycling will differ from one ecosystem to another. The first investigation described below may help you understand this process.

1. To compare the organic content of a bog soil (peat) with a woodland or grassland soil

Introduction
This study will help us make some comment on nutrient cycling in a bog. We will compare the amount of dead organic matter (non-decomposed) found in the soil of two different

ecosystems. Take a bog as one of these ecosystems and say a woodland or grassland as another.

Equipment:
Field: Soil auger (or trowel), plastic/polythene bags and labels.

Laboratory: Electronic balance, drying oven (40°C), numbered soil trays, safety spectacles, bunsen, tripod, pipe-clay triangle, clamp, crucible, matches and a mortar and pestle.

Method:
Field: Choose one site per group (of at least two) in each ecosystem. Take a core 25 cm deep of the soil below the living plants. Place the sample in a polythene bag, seal and label it.

Laboratory: Use data sheets similar to those in Table 1 and Table 2 in Appendix 6 to record your results. Mix the soil samples thoroughly in their bags. Choose a sub-sample of each soil type (enough to fill a crucible). Weigh in a pre-weighed soil tin. Note the number. Dry the sample in the oven at 40°C for 1 hour. Re-weigh the sample and tin. Make a note of the result.

Break up the dried sample using the mortar and pestle and place in a crucible. Wearing safety spectacles heat the samples. The samples are ready when the soil has become ash-like. What do you notice about the bog samples? Using a clamp, carefully place the contents into the correctly numbered soil tin. Let it cool slightly before weighing. The sample should ideally be cooled in a desiccator. Weigh the sample. Calculate the % moisture content and the % organic content and tabulate your results. The formulas for these calculations are given in Appendix 6. Take the average (mean) figures for each ecosystem.

Use your results to answer the following questions: 1. Which samples had the largest proportion of organic matter? 2. Which samples had the largest amount of moisture? 3. What can you say about the rates of decomposition in the two ecosystems? 4. What might prevent or slow down the process of decomposition? 5. What effect would a high moisture content have on decomposition?

2. Analysis of vegetation: To compare the flora of a wet area of bog with that of cutaway bog

Introduction
This study compares two different areas of vegetation on a bog. The types and frequencies of plants and other organisms that grow in an ecosystem are influenced by factors that affect the place or habitat in which they live. These conditions in which they live (their environment) may be divided into non-living (abiotic) and living (biotic) environments. Examples of abiotic or physical environmental factors are temperature, water, light, humidity, wind, pH, mineral salts and trace elements. Examples of biotic environmental factors are predation, competition and population density.

In this investigation you will see whether there are differences in the presence and distribution of plant species within a wet area of bog (the bog proper) and a dry area of bog (the cutaway area surrounding the bog). Ideally a study of environmental factors should be undertaken with this study so as to interpret differences in the species composition of the vegetation in the two areas. For example you could measure moisture and organic content of the soil, human influence and soil temperature.

Equipment:
Field: 1 X 1 m quadrat, labels for unidentified plants, polythene bags, clipboard and pencil, a field data sheet similar to that in Table 3 in Appendix 6 and a book which will help you identify plants—preferably a plant key.

Choice of sites: For the bog proper make sure you choose a wet area, ideally with a well developed hummock and hollow system. Randomly sample within the area. In the case of the cutaway bog, work back from the peat face.

Method:
Field: A random sampling method is chosen for this investigation. Throw the quadrat over your shoulder and record the plant species present in your sample area on the data sheet. Use one data sheet for each area. Tick off each species present under the appropriate quadrat number. Add additional species as you find them. If you cannot identify a species take a sample, label and place it in a bag to be identified later. In the meantime call it some name to help you remember it should you find it in another quadrat.

Try to complete about 10 samples in each area. If you come as a class group divide into groups of 3 or 4 and collect more samples.

Laboratory: Try to identify any plants you brought back and put the correct names on the data sheet. Work out the frequency of each species in both areas using the formula given in Appendix 6. These results may be summarised by producing a table with the % frequency of each species in both areas (see Table 4 Appendix 6).

When studying the results use these questions as guidelines: 1. Do you notice any difference in species composition between the two areas? 2. Which plants are exclusive to each of your areas? 3. Which plants have a high frequency in each area? 4. What environmental factors do you think might govern the differences in species composition?

3. A survey of freshwater invertebrates

Introduction
At first sight it is difficult to believe that a bog pool contains much animal life. However, a brief sampling period should produce a variety of animals. An important question to ask is how do the animals obtain food to give them energy? What do they eat? The animals of bog pools fall into two main categories: those eating plant life which are known as herbivores or primary consumers and those that eat the herbivores which are known as carnivores or secondary consumers. In addition there are carnivores that eat other carnivores and so on. A nutritional sequence of different organisms will form a food chain with each link in the sequence representing a trophic (feeding) level. You are likely to find a food web in the bog pool where there are a number of different types of organism at any one trophic level. We eat food from a variety of sources to obtain energy. In the same way the animals in the bog pool may feed on different types of organisms at lower trophic levels. Their nutritional relationships may be represented in a food web.

Equipment:
Field: sweep nets, sorting trays, pipette, tweezers, forceps, various sized jars and a magnifying glass.

Method:
Choose the largest bog pool you can find. It is best to pick a pool in the cutaway area around the bog where you can see that the sides are solid. Fill the sorting trays with water. Using your sweep net sample the bog water and the material at the bottom of the pool. The best sampling technique is to jiggle the net up and down as you sweep through the water. This is really necessary if your bog pool contains a lot of vegetation. Put your sample in a tray and wash the net in the tray. Let the sediment settle. Examine what you have caught, using a magnifying glass if necessary. Sort the different organisms into jars. Try to identify them using the lists and illustrations in this book or any suitable book listed in the Further Reading chapter. Try to find out what you can about the organisms at the site and return them to the pool. If possible make a count of the number of each type of organism that you find and list them. When you get back to the laboratory, use reference books to find out about their feeding habits and life cycles. Try to work out the feeding relationships between the different organisms you have found. Sort them into Primary Consumers (C1), which are herbivores, Secondary (C2) and Tertiary (C3) Consumers which are both carnivores.

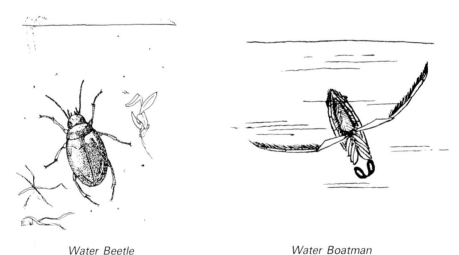

Water Beetle   *Water Boatman*

1. How many trophic levels have you found? 2. Can you form a food web with your results? 3. Is there a difference in the abundance of organisms at each trophic level?

The investigations presented above are simple and will tell you something about the ecology of a bog. However, the aspects covered could be studied in more detail and the techniques presented could be expanded upon should you wish to do so. Other possible experiments could include a comparison of various abiotic factors within a soil profile from a bog and a woodland or grassland and studies of terrestrial invertebrate populations of bogs to name but two.

WHAT FUTURE FOR OUR BOGS?

Peter Foss

This book has dealt with many aspects of peatlands, and various authors have discussed the specialised assemblage of animals and plants found in these habitats. The amazing preserving powers of bogs have been described in the archaeology section. We have also seen how peatlands have been a source of inspiration to the higher creative senses of the Irish people for generations, right up to the present day. The wide range of practical uses to which bogs have been put have been described, the oldest and best known being the use of peat for fuel in the home which has created a strong bond between man and bog. It is not surprising that peatlands are rightly regarded by many as a very unique Irish ecosystem, and some at least are surely worthy of conservation as a specialised ecosystem composed of many uniquely adapted plants and animals.

One area which has been given little consideration is the value, in financial terms of conserved, rather than exploited peatlands. This does not imply that the economic value of turf exploitation is being regarded solely in a negative way by conservationists. The work of the larger state agencies, such as Bord na Móna and the Forestry Service play an important role in the economic functioning of this country. That both of these agencies have been able to create so much wealth, from what is in effect 98 % water is truly commendable. However the desire to increase profits should not occur without any regard for our conservation needs. Conservation and exploitation have and can occur side by side without antagonism.

Such co-operation is all the more important because in the 1980's Ireland's revenue from tourism has been growning steadily to become one of the country's major sources of income. Tourists come to Ireland to enjoy our Irish hospitality and unspoilt environment. In contrast to many western European countries Ireland still boasts a relatively natural, clean, unspoilt environment. Bogs, and in particular blanket bog is a major attraction to tourists in the west of Ireland—but how much longer will this be the case? At the present rate of exploitation, some of these highly sought after recreational areas may be extinct by the 1990's. What will attract tourists when the Atlantic seaboard is dominated by one vast carpet of conifers, or worse still is turned into a black desert? Are we not taking a very short term view of the potential value of this resource to the country? This is not to say that exploitation should be completely stopped—rather a number of selected areas should be conserved and managed for tourism—one of our few "boom" industries.

To continue as an attractive holiday destination we require more than just the creation of a more aggressive tourist board—we must have a co-ordinated plan for our environment which considers more than just short term economic gains. Tourism is a renewable resource (if we play our cards right!) that should be given greater consideration when planning the development of our unspoilt environment.

We are obliged to conserve peatlands for future generations so that they too can profit from this national resource. This resource has a far greater potential than we are led to believe by the short-sighted exploiters. Certainly conservation requires financial backing—a facility that has always been made readily available to peat exploitation agencies, who argue in favour of cash support to produce a short term profit. By the same token, conservation could provide the same if not an even greater financial return to the Irish nation, and go on doing so long after the cutaway bogs are gone. Not only would such a measure benefit us in economic terms, but we would also be safeguarding part of our natural heritage—peatlands have a greater potential than is usually portrayed.

Why then is funding not made available, even on a much smaller scale, to the state agencies responsible for conserving our peatland heritage? We cannot blame this lack of financial support for conservation on our poor economic standing at the present time. Most peatland exploitation agencies are presently in receipt of substantial funding from state and foreign agencies. Why then does conservation not get the recognition it deserves from planners?

What seems to be missing is a sense of national pride in our peatlands—an Irish landscape feature. Since peatlands are central to our Irish identity, they should be regarded as beautiful and their worth acknowledged by a determination to conserve them. Our unwillingness to change our attitudes may in fact be blinding us as to the real economic potential of conserved bogs.

Europeans are enthralled by the peatlands they see in Ireland, and their spending proves it. Many others have learned from their mistakes and are anxious to see some of these areas conserved. Why don't we act now before the bogs are gone for ever and it is too late? When the last bog is destroyed, it will take hundreds of generations before they can rise again—must we make future generations wait that long to experience the beauty of the peatland wilderness that we are still lucky enough to have today?

PEATLANDS TO VISIT IN THE REPUBLIC OF IRELAND

Catherine O'Connell

If contemplating a visit to any of the peatland sites listed below we would ask you to remember that Irish peatlands are endangered habitats, sensitive to human disturbance. If conserved and protected peatlands are to retain their beauty and scientific value, everyone who uses them for recreational or educational purposes must take care. Your visit to a peatland should do nothing to interfere with the conservation value of the site or with the enjoyment of the site by others. We ask you to follow the *Country Code*.

1. Respect the rights of landowners. Seek permission before crossing fields to get to peatlands.

2. Close gates securely if you open them.

3. Do not damage fences, hedges or walls.

4. Absolutely *no* fires.

5. Leave no litter.

6. Do not pick plants or disturb wild animals and birds or their nests at any peatland site.

7. Peatlands can be dangerous places, never visit them alone.

Each of the sites is listed by name, county and the national grid reference, according to the half inch ordnance survey maps of Ireland. The locations of all of the sites are indicated in (Figure 15).

1. Scragh Bog, County Westmeath (N4259)
Scragh Bog is a small but extremely wet quaking fen with an area of 16 ha. The site is of international importance. Several rare plant and moss species are found here. There are a number of distinct habitats to be seen ranging from areas of open water to fen woodland. Most of the fen is owned by the Irish Peatland Conservation Council. It is our intention to hand this site over to the Government to be managed by the Forest and Wildlife Service as a National Nature Reserve.

The fen is situated 7 km north-west of Mullingar. Take the main Sligo road from Mullingar (N4). After the level crossing, take the second turn right (eastwards). The fen lies 1.5 km along this small road. If visiting this area, there is no right of way to the fen. Permission to cross fields must be sought from the local farmer. Extreme caution should be exercised in getting onto the fen. At the edges an unstable quaking mat of vegetation must be crossed before getting to the middle of the fen which is more solid under foot. The nearest tourist office is in Mullingar.

2. Mongan Bog, County Offaly (N0330)
Mongan Bog is an internationally important raised bog with an area of 150 ha. The surface of the bog has a well developed hummock and pool system. The Greenland White-fronted Geese use this bog as a winter roosting site. The bog will be conserved and managed by An Taisce and is scheduled to become a National Nature Reserve. Mongan Bog is part of the Clonmacnoise Heritage Zone. This area includes the Monastic site at Clonmacnoise which is managed by the Office of Public Works, Fin Lough, eskers and a section of the Shannon callows. The Heritage Zone offers visitors the chance to explore a wide variety of habitats besides the bog, all within a small area.

Mongan Bog lies 2 km east of Clonmacnoise between two esker ridges. Intending visitors should seek permission from An Taisce at Tailors Hall. Approaching from the N6, the main Dublin to Athlone road, any of the third class roads sign-posted to Clonmacnoise lead to the southern margin of the bog. The best access is near a lay-by on the road at the western section of the bog. There is a tourist office at Clonmacnoise.

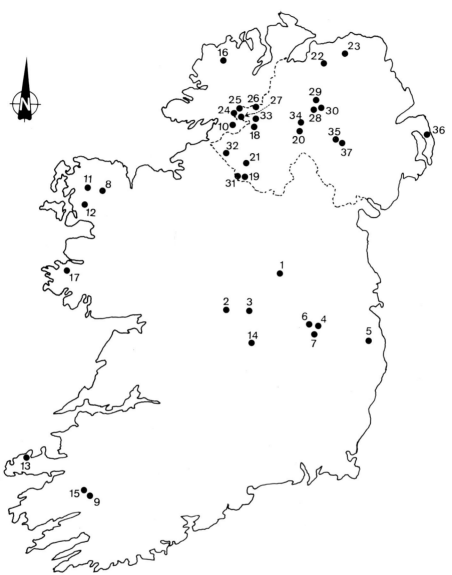

Figure 15—Map showing the location of the peatlands to visit. The location of each peatland referred to in the chapters on Places to Visit are indicated. Each site is identified according to a number. 1. Scragh Bog, 2. Mongan Bog, 3. Clara Bog, 4. Mouds Bog, 5. Sallygap, 6. Peatland Interpretation Centre, 7. Pollardstown Fen NNR, 8. Owenboy NNR, 9. Owenreagh Valley NNR, 10. Pettigo Plateau NNR, 11. Knockmoyle/Sheskin NNR, 12. Owenduff, 13. Mount Brandon NNR, 14. Slieve Blooms NNR, 15. Killarney National Park, 16. Glenveagh National Park, 17. Connemara National Park, 18. Aghagrefin, 19. Aghatirourke, 20. Black Bog, 21. Bolusty Beg, 22. Craig-Na-Shoke, 23. Garry Bog, 24. & 25. Killeter Forest Goose Lawns, 26. Moneygal Bog, 27. Mullyfamore, 28. & 29. Slaghtfreedan, 30. Teal Lough, 31. Crossmurrin NNR, 32. Lough Naman Bog NNR, 33. Meenadoan NNR, 34. The Murrins NNR, 35. The Argory Mosses, 36. Inishargy Bog and 37. Peatlands Country Park.

3. Clara Bog, County Offaly (N2530)

Clara Bog is an internationally important raised bog. It is one of the largest raised bogs remaining with an area of 665 ha. It is the only raised bog in Ireland that has a well developed soak system. In addition to the soak areas the bog has a well developed hummock and hollow topography.

Since 1983, one half of the bog has been drained by Bord na Móna, who acquired it for peat extraction. In 1986 the Government committed itself to conserving this bog. It will be managed as a National Nature Reserve by the Forest and Wildlife Service.

The bog lies 2 km south of Clara town on either side of the road to Rahan. Access to Clara itself is along the L113. It is hoped that an Interpretive Centre will be opened in Clara town in the near future. The nearest tourist office is at Clonmacnoise.

4. Mouds Bog, County Kildare (N7818)

Mouds Bog is one of the largest (526 ha) and most easterly raised bogs in Ireland. Although the surface of the bog is relatively dry, due to burning and cutting, there are areas where the typical raised bog hummock and hollow topography can be seen. In a wet depression close to the eastern margin of the bog a colony of Pitcher Plants can be seen.

The bog is privately owned and is located 48 km from Dublin. Intending visitors should seek permission to visit the site from the local farmers. The proximity to the city makes it one of the easiest sites to visit. The bog lies 4 km north-west of Newbridge. As you enter the town along the N7, take the third class road which runs parallel to the river Liffey just after you cross the bridge. Follow this road for 1.5 km or until you reach the third sign-posted turn to the left (westwards). This leads to the bog. The Bord na Móna Library and a tourist office are both located in Newbridge. There is a Peatland Interpretation Centre at Lullymore where further information and exhibits can be seen.

5. Sallygap, County Wicklow (O1413)

Sallygap is an internationally important mountain blanket bog area, covering 1,700 ha. This area of blanket bog is the least damaged in the eastern part of the country. All of the typical mountain blanket bog features can be seen, such as lakes, pools and surface drains. This peatland area has come under increasing threat in recent years as peat cutting has intensified particularly in the western section.

The area is privately owned but there are plans to protect part of the area within a National Park. It lies 22 km south of Dublin. This makes it a popular site for many Dubliners and ideal for educational outings. Take the L94 from Dublin to the Sallygap. Further information can be obtained from tourist offices in Dublin or Bray. For those interested in spending the weekend, there is an An Oige youth hostel in Glencree.

6. Peatland Interpretation Centre, Lullymore, County Kildare (N704264)

The Peatland Interpretation Centre at Lullymore is to be opened during 1988. Located near Robertstown in a research station run by An Foras Taluntais, the centre is situated in the heart of the Bog of Allen. This extensive peatland area has been developed by Bord na Móna for the last 25 years.

A display room in the Interpretation Centre will contain a series of models, explaining the development, wildlife and use of Irish bogs. Guided excursions will be organised (by prior appointment) to introduce participants to various aspects of peatland ecology, conservation and exploitation and to examine the agricultural potential of cutaway bog.

The centre will be open during the summer season. However, arrangements can be made for visiting school groups during the winter. Picnic facilities are being arranged.

The Peatland Interpretation Centre is located south-west of Dublin and can be reached by car on the L2 trunk route via Celbridge, Clane, Prosperous and Allenwood. It is convenient to the Kildare Way and the Canal Way, walking and boating routes respectively. Further information can be obtained from An Foras Taluntais.

National Nature Reserves

There are currently seven peatlands in Ireland which are National Nature Reserves (NNRs) These are owned and managed by the Forest and Wildlife Service (FWS). They are protected under the Wildlife Act 1976. Maps of all of the sites are available from the Stationary Office. There are no facilities at the sites and no restrictions to access but visitors are asked to obey the Country Code.

7. Pollardstown Fen NNR, County Kildare (N7716)

Pollardstown Fen is the largest remaining calcareous, spring-fed fen in Ireland. It has an area of 225 ha and is of international importance. In the past attempts were made to reclaim the centre of the fen. This area (of 130 ha) was recently purchased by the FWS who have reflooded it to encourage regeneration of fen vegetation. Thus there is a large body of open water in the centre of the fen. One immediate result of the flooding is that the site has become increasingly important for wildfowl. Surrounding the flooded area is the typical undisturbed fen vegetation some of which is still privately owned. Here the plants and animals so characteristic of this rich habitat can be found.

The proximity of this site to Dublin, (48 km), makes it ideal for day visits and educational outings. The fen lies 3 km north-east of Newbridge. Take the N7 from Newbridge to Kildare for 3 km until you reach the Curragh. Take the third class road to the right which runs parallel to the racecourse. Take the first right followed by the first left over the railway. Drive for 1 km until you reach a concealed laneway on the right hand side at a bend in the road. The entrance to the fen is at the bottom of the laneway. The Bord na Móna Library and the nearest tourist office are in Newbridge. At the Peatland Interpretation Centre in Lullymore exhibits can be seen.

8. Owenboy NNR, County Mayo (G0516)

This peatland area of 480 ha is of international scientific importance. There are extensive areas of Atlantic blanket bog vegetation and a number of domes which support vegetation more typical of raised bogs. Within the area there is a network of mineral rich flushes which have an interesting moss flora. The site is used by Greenland White-fronted Geese.

The bog is located approximately 10 km west of Crossmolina and 10 km east of Bellacorick on the southern side of the Ballina to Belmullet road (T58) at Eskeragh Bridge. Access to the site is from the minor road off the T58, 1 km west of Eskeragh Bridge. The nearest tourist office is in Ballina.

9. Owenreagh Valley (Eirk) NNR, County Kerry (V8678)

This is a small but intact bog of international importance. The total area of the site is 72 ha, 16 ha of which are owned by the FWS. The bog has developed in the floodplain of the Owenreagh river. The morphology and vegetation of the bog is intermediate between raised and Atlantic blanket bog. There are eight domes on the bog which support vegetation typical of raised bogs. These are separated by streams containing fen vegetation. The lower slopes of the valley side support a mosaic of different vegetation types including wet heath, patches of blanket bog and remnants of woodland.

The bog is situated in the Owenreagh valley approximately 1 km north of Moll's Gap. Access to the site is from the third class road, north of Moll's Gap, which runs parallel to the Owenreagh river. There is a youth hostel in Gearhameen and the nearest tourist offices are in Kenmare and Killarney.

10. Pettigo Plateau NNR, County Donegal (H0274)

Pettigo Plateau, comprising 900 ha is an excellent example of the typical intact Donegal Atlantic blanket bog. It is a site of national importance. The bog is surrounded by a number of large lakes including the Dunragh Loughs, L. Barderg and part of L. Golagh. There are numerous pools and some drainage features to be seen. It is in this habitat that the Greenland White-fronted Geese winter. This blanket bog area also encompasses a number of other interesting habitats including wet heaths, raised bog domes and lakes.

The bog lies to the west of Lough Derg approximately 10 km from Donegal town. Access to the site is on foot from the T35 along a new forest road, west of Farbreagagh Hill. The nearest tourist office is in Donegal town.

11. Knockmoyle/Sheskin NNR, County Mayo (F9825)
An extensive area (732 ha) of Atlantic blanket bog. A number of tributaries of the Oweniny river flow through the bog in shallow valleys. These arise as flushed areas from a ridge to the north of the bog, and run in a north-south direction. The blanket bog between the streams is wet and contains numerous pools and lakes.

The area lies to the north of the Bord na Móna works at Bellacorick, between the Oweniny river on the eastern side and Sheskin Lodge and the ruined settlement of Sheskin on the western side. Access to the site is from the T58, along a minor road adjacent to the Bellacorick power station or from the ruins at Sheskin. The nearest tourist office is in Ballina.

12. Owenduff, County Mayo (F8607)
This is an extensive area of Atlantic blanket bog with a total area of 6,000 ha. A large portion of the area (1,700 ha) is owned by FWS and is scheduled to become an NNR. The area is of international importance as it is the largest remaining undistrubed blanket bog catchment in the country. A mosaic of different habitats are found here including blanket bog, mountain heath, lakes, streams and rivers. The area is an important roosting and feeding site for Greenland White-fronted Geese.

The area lies west of Nephin Beg and 6 km east of the T71, the road linking Mallaranny to Bangor. If travelling to the site, take the T71 from Mallaranny to Bellaveeny. At Bellaveeny, take the third class road due north to Bellagarvaun. Follow the track eastwards to Srahduggaun. This takes you to the section owned by FWS. The nearest tourist offices are in Westport and Castlebar.

13. Mount Brandon NNR, County Kerry (Q4611)
An extensive area (4,000 ha) of mountain blanket bog with cliffs at higher levels. A portion of this area (461 ha), south of the sea cliffs is owned by the FWS.

Access to the site is from the third class road north of Dingle. The nearest tourist office is in Dingle.

14. Slieve Blooms NNR, Counties Laois and Offaly (N2510)
The Slieve Bloom area contains an internationally important mountain blanket bog, areas of heathland, including the headwaters of a number of small streams. This complex of habitats covers an area of 2,100 ha and is part of an Environmental Park that is being developed in the area.

There are a number of access points recognisable by the green signs, either from the T9 linking Tullamore to Roscrea or from the N5 from Portlaoise to Roscrea. Within these mountains there are extensive areas of Pine and Spruce plantations where there are picnic facilities and forest walks. There are at least 4 scenic routes over the mountains, but for the "bog trotters" the best one is the Cut. This route begins 8 km south of Clonaslee on the third class road to Mountrath. It allows access to Wolftrap Mountain and an area of intact mountain blanket bog. The nearest tourist offices are in Birr and Portlaoise.

PEATLANDS IN THE NATIONAL PARKS

Alan Craig

Three national parks, wholly owned by the State, have been established and are managed by the National Parks and Monuments Service of the Office of Public Works. Their twin aims are to protect the outstanding natural features within their boundaries and to enable people to appreciate and enjoy this natural heritage. All three are in the region of western Ireland where blanket bogs occur right down to sea level, and in all of them blanket bogs and wet heathland are the most widespread vegetation. Educational visits by schools and clubs are welcomed. The locations of the National Parks are indicated in Figure 15.

15. Killarney National Park, County Kerry (V9786)

Killarney National Park (incorporating the Bourn Vincent Memorial Park) comprises 10,000 ha of mountains, moorland, woods and lakes. There are several quite distinct types of bog and heathland. Interesting bogs include Newfoundland Bog on a low-lying rocky peninsula by Killarney's Upper Lake, bogs rich in Deer Sedge on the hills which are grazed throughout the year by a herd of native Red Deer and bogs with Crowberry and other mountain plants high on Mangerton Mountain. Greater Butterwort, an insectivorous bog plant mainly found on mountains from northern Spain to the western Alps is common here.

Visitor services include an audio-visual introduction to the park, shown in the main visitor centre at Muckross House, and a general guide-book on sale there and in other information offices. Muckross House is 5 km south of Killarney off the Killarney to Kenmare road (N71), which continues through the park close to all the main peatland areas.

16. Glenveagh National Park, County Donegal (C0422)

Glenveagh National Park comprises 10,000 ha of virtual wilderness in the heart of the mountains of north-west Donegal. The bog and heathland vegetation is quite similar to that of Killarney. Derrybeg Bog in a beautiful location behind a sandy beach at the head of Lough Veagh, is a nationally important bog, in appearance quite like a midland raised bog but with blanket bog vegetation. Bogs and wet heaths extend up to the rounded summits of the granite mountains.

Services in the visitor centre include an audio-visual introduction to the park and extensive displays with one room devoted specifically to mountains and moorlands. Visitors can see peatlands at first hand on the Derrylahan nature trail or on guided walks during the summer. The park entrance is about 22 km from Letterkenny on the road (L74) to Gweedore. There is an An Óige Youth Hostel at Dunlewy.

17. Connemara National Park, County Galway (L7357)

Connemara National Park comprises 2,000 ha of hills, valleys and rocky peaks on the northern side of the Twelve Bens mountain range in County Galway. Almost the whole of the park is covered by blanket bog and heath. The peatland flora includes St. Dabeoc's Heath which grows in the Atlantic fringe of south-west Europe as well as Connemara.

Visitor services include an audio-visual introduction to the park and a photographic exhibition both of which highlight the area's peatlands. Bogs can be seen at first hand on the Sruffaunboy nature trail or on guided walks during the summer. Access to the park is just west of Letterfrack on the Clifden to Leenane road (N59).

A small part of the rocky lake-strewn blanket bog between Roundstone and Clifden, which is an internationally important area, has been acquired as part of plans for a future southern unit of Connemara National Park, but no visitor services are possible at present.

PEATLANDS TO VISIT IN NORTHERN IRELAND

David Dunlop

The principle concentrations of raised bogs in Northern Ireland are located along the valleys of the Lower River Bann (Counties Antrim and Derry) and the Fairy Water (County Tyrone). Most of the bogs are in private ownership and not open to the general public. There was once a large raised bog system to the south of Lough Neagh in County Armagh but much of this has been cut away and reclaimed for agriculture.

Extensive areas of mountain blanket bog occur on the Antrim Plateau (County Antrim), the Sperrin Mountains (Counties Tyrone and Derry) and the Cuilcagh Mountains (County Fermanagh).

All of the National Nature Reserves (NNRs) and some Forest Nature Reserves are marked on the Northern Ireland Ordnance Survey maps. At all of the sites described the relevant sheet numbers are included. The locations of all of the sites are indicated on Figure 15.

Forest Nature Reserves

These are owned and managed by the Forest Service of the Department of Agriculture (DoA) for Northern Ireland. There are no facilities on any of these reserves and no restrictions on access. Further information and detailed directions on how to get to the sites listed below is available from the DoA.

18. Aghagrefin, County Fermanagh (H210657)

A regenerating cutaway bog of 40 ha. Access to the site is from the north and west boundaries from the public road off the B4 near Ederny, see Sheet 17. The nearest tourist office is in Enniskillen. The site is best visited from May to July. There are a wide variety of Sedges and Bog Mosses to be seen, as well as Bulrush, Water Horsetail and areas of Birch woodland. A number of birds such as Mallard, Snipe and Woodcock can be seen in winter.

19. Aghatirourke, County Fermanagh (H161315)

This area of 695 ha includes bog, limestone and archaeological sites. Access to the site is from the north-east on foot from Florence Court Forest Park, or from the public car park at Gortaloughany, see Sheet 26. The nearest tourist office is in Enniskillen. The area is best visited in spring and summer. The upper part extending south-west to the summit of Cuilcagh (684 m) is blanket bog with a typical flora.

20. Black Bog, County Tyrone (H642812)

This is a raised bog of 48 ha. It is one of the largest intact raised bogs in Northern Ireland. Features to be seen include pool and hummock complexes and an infilled bog lake. The Marsh Fritillary and Green Hairstreak Butterflies are found here. Access to the site is across country from the public road to the north, off the B46, see Sheet 13. The nearest tourist office is in Omagh.

21. Bolusty Beg, County Fermanagh (H050569)

A small bog of 6.8 ha. Hummocks of Silver-haired Moss and pools rich in Bog Moss with a variety of Sundews can be seen. There is no restriction on access which is on foot from the forest road in Lough Navar Forest off the B99. The site is sign-posted "Lough Navar Forest Park" from Derrygonnelly, see Sheet 17. The nearest tourist office is in Enniskillen. There are scenic drives in this area.

22. Craig-Na-Shoke, County Derry (C746005)

This is an area of mountain blanket bog (90 ha). At the highest part of the reserve on Mullaghmore (560 m) bog erosion features can be seen such as peat "haggs" and erosion channels. Access to the site is on foot via the forest road off a minor road, off the B40 between Draperstown and Feeny, see Sheet 8. The nearest tourist office is in Strabane.

23. Garry Bog, County Antrim (C938298)

A small raised bog of 6.5 ha. Typical bog plants can be seen. Access to the site is from the public road to the west, off the B66 near Ballymoney, see Sheet 8. The nearest tourist office is in Ballycastle.

24. & 25. Killeter Forest Goose Lawns, County Tyrone (H093798 & H078826)

Two areas of mountain blanket bog covering 15.8 ha. This area is best visited from December to March. Greenland White-fronted Geese feed on the White Beak Sedge in winter which occurs on this site. Access to the site is via the forest road on foot, in Killeter Forest off minor roads off the B72 near Castlederg, see Sheet 12. The nearest tourist office is in Strabane.

26. Moneygal Bog, County Tyrone (H241880)

An intact raised bog of 47 ha with a well developed dome. Large hummocks of Bog Moss occur here. Mallard, Golden Plover, Redshank, Snipe and Jack Snipe have been recorded from the site. Access to the site is from minor roads off the B72 near Castlederg, see Sheet 12. The nearest tourist office is in Strabane.

27. Mullyfamore, County Tyrone (H105797)

A small raised bog of 13.2 ha, with a well developed pool and hummock complex. This bog is a known winter feeding station for Greenland White-fronted Geese. Access to the site is from minor roads and forest roads in Killeter Forest near Castlederg, see Sheet 12. The nearest tourist office is in Strabane.

28. & 29. Slaghtfreedan, County Tyrone (H728859 & H735862)

Two very low lying raised bogs (18.6 ha) with pool and hummock complexes. Access to the bog is on foot via the forest road to the south-east in Davagh Forest Park from minor roads off the B162, north of Cookstown, see Sheet 13. The area is sign-posted "Davagh Forest". The western edge of this site is bounded by Golan Water, much frequented by wildfowl in winter. The nearest tourist office is in Omagh.

30. Teal Lough, County Tyrone (H731880)

A small raised bog of 40 ha, with a well developed pool and hummock complex. This area is a known nesting site for Black-headed Gulls and Teal. A variety of wildfowl visit the area in winter. Access to the site is from minor roads off the B162, north of Cookstown, see Sheet 13. The nearest tourist office is in Omagh.

National Nature Reserves (NNRs)

These are owned or leased by the Department of the Environment (DoE) for Northern Ireland and are managed by their Countryside and Wildlife Branch. The sites have been rated in the United Kingdom as of national or international importance. Persons wishing to visit any of these sites should contact the Countryside and Wildlife Branch at Calvert House and they will put you in contact with the Reserve Warden for the site.

31. Crossmurrin NNR, County Fermanagh (H112348)

This reserve mostly covers limestone pavement, but a small area of blanket bog is included. Access to the site is from Marlbank scenic road, near Belcoo, see Sheet 26. The nearest tourist office is in Enniskillen.

24. & 25. Killeter NNR, County Tyrone (H093798 & H078826)

This reserve is also a Forest Nature Reserve and is described under that category.

32. Lough Naman Bog NNR, County Fermanagh (H026525)

A large tract of blanket bog with well developed hummock and hollow communities. Access to the site is off the minor road from Derrygonnelly to Garrison via Glennasheevar, see Sheet 17. The nearest tourist office is in Enniskillen.

33. Meenadoan NNR, County Tyrone (H244718)

A small bog with a typical flora and fauna. Access is from the road between Drumquin and Pettigo, west of Lough Bradan Forest, see Sheet 12. The nearest tourist office is in Strabane.

34. The Murrins NNR, County Tyrone (H565780)

An area of mountain blanket bog including some wet heathland. Access to the site is near Mountfield village, see Sheet 13. The nearest tourist office is in Omagh.

Ulster Trust for Nature Conservation Nature Reserves

These sites are leased by the Ulster Trust for Nature Conservation (UTNC), a voluntary and charitable body which manages them to maintain or enhance their nature conservation value. Intending visitors who are not members of the UTNC should seek permission from the UTNC headquarters before travelling to the reserves. Brochures for these reserves are in preparation and will be available from the UTNC.

35. The Argory Mosses, County Armagh (H8757 and H8857)

This site consists of the High Moss (10 ha) and the Low Moss (7 ha). The High Moss is to be retained as a raised bog system with associated flora. The Low Moss will be allowed to continue its succession from cutaway bog to Birch dominated woodland. Access to the site is from The Argory, a National Trust property, which is sign-posted from where the B131 leaves the M1 at junction 13, see Sheet 19. The nearest tourist office is in Banbridge.

36. Inishargy Bog, County Down (J615645)

A small (4 ha) inter-drumlin cutaway bog. The site comprises bog and fen with Alder and Willow carr. Access to the site is 2 km north east of Kircubbin, off a minor road, see Sheet 21. The nearest tourist offices are in Bangor and Belfast.

Country Parks

Country Parks are owned or leased by the Department of the Environment and are managed by their Countryside and Wildlife Branch. They are intended to educate the public about their environment and provide places for recreation in the countryside.

37. Peatlands Country Park, The Birches, County Armagh (H9061)

This park contains extensive areas of cutaway bog and wooded drumlins. The area is being developed for passive recreation and to educate the public about all aspects of peatland ecology and exploitation. It includes two adjacent NNRs: Mullenakill and Annagarriff. These reserves illustrate aspects of bog development and native woodland. Many rare plants occur in the area which also has a high entomological value. The site is open to the public although it has not been officially opened as yet. Access is north of the Loughgall exit on the M1 motorway. If you wish to have a guided tour or visit the National Nature Reserves adjacent please contact the Warden, Mr Keith Stanfield, 19 Old Kilmore Road, Moira, Craigavon BT67 0LZ or DoE Countryside and Wildlife Branch.

SOURCES OF FURTHER INFORMATION

An Foras Forbartha, St. Martins House, Waterloo Road, Ballsbridge, Dublin 4. 602511

An Foras Talúntais, Headquarters, 19 Sandymount Avenue, Ballsbridge, Dublin 4. 688188

Clara Development Association, c/o Mr Michael Petit, The Square, Clara, Co. Offaly.

Irish Youth Hostel Association, An Óige, 39 Mountjoy Square, Dublin 1. 364750/363111

An Taisce, Tailors Hall, Back Lane, Dublin 8. 541786

Bord Fáilte, Baggot Street Bridge, Dublin 2. 765871

Bord Na Móna, 76 Lower Baggot Street, Dublin 2. 688555

Cospoir Long Distance Walking Routes Committee, Floor 11, Hawkins House, Dublin 2. 714311 ext. 102

Department of Agriculture for Northern Ireland, Forest Service, Headquarters, Dundonald House, Upper Newtownards Road, Belfast. 650111

Department of the Environment for Northern Ireland, Countryside and Wildlife Branch, Calvert House, 23 Castle Place, Belfast BT1 1FY. 230560.

Dutch Foundation for the Conservation of Irish Bogs, 52 Hugo de Grootstraat, 6522 DG Nijmegen, Netherlands. 235191

Environment Awareness Bureau, 5 Wilton Place, Dublin 2. 763368/763369

Government Publications Sales Office, Sun Alliance House, Molesworth Street, Dublin 2. 710309

Irish Peatland Conservation Council, 195 Pearse Street, Dublin 2.

Irish Ramblers Club, 27 Newbride Street, Dublin 8.

Irish Wildbird Conservancy, Southview, Church Road, Greystones, Co. Wicklow. 875759

Irish Wildlife Federation, 132A East Wall Road, Dublin 3.

National Association of Regional Game Councils, Growtown, Porterstown Lane, Dunshaughlin, Co. Meath.

Nature Conservancy Council, Northminster House, Peterborough PE1 1UA, England.

Northern Ireland Tourist Board, River House, High Street, Belfast. 246609

Office of Public Works, National Parks and Monuments Service, 51 St. Stephens Green, Dublin 2. 613111

Peatland Interpretation Centre, An Foras Talúntais, Peatland Experimental Station, Lullymore, Co. Kildare. 60133

Royal Society for the Protection of Birds, Belvoir Forest Park, Belfast. 692547

Ulster Trust for Nature Conservation, Barnetts' Cottage, Barnett Demesne, Malone Road, Belfast BT9 5PB. 612235

Wildlife Advisory Council, Leeson Lane, Dublin 2. 615666

Wildlife Service, Leeson Lane, Dublin 2. 615666

Youth Information Centre, Sackville House, Sackville Place, Dublin 1. 786844

FURTHER READING

Allen, G. & Denslow, J. (1970) *Freshwater Animals*. The Clue Books, Oxford University Press.

Anonymous (1976) *Wetlands Discovered*. Forest & Wildlife Service, Dublin.

Anonymous (1976) *Wildlife and the Law*. A Guide to the Wildlife Act 1976. Stationary Office, Dublin.

Anonymous (1977) *Nature Conservation and Agriculture*. Appraisal and proposals by the Nature Conservancy Council. Nature Conservancy Council, London.

Anonymous (1981) *Areas of Scientific Interest in Ireland*. An Foras Forbartha, Dublin.

Anonymous (1982) The Conservation of Peat Bogs. Interpretive Branch, Nature Conservancy Council, Peterborough.

Anonymous (1983) The Conservation of Mountain and Moorland. Interpretive Branch, Nature Conservancy Council, Peterborough.

Anonymous (1983) The Conservation of Fens and Marshes. Interpretive Branch, Nature Conservancy Council, Peterborough.

Anonymous (1986) Irish Peatland Conservation Council Action Plan 1987-1989. IPCC, Dublin.

Bellamy, D. (1986) *The Wild Boglands — Bellamy's Ireland*. Country House, Dublin.

Christie, S.J. (1986) Peatlands of Northern Ireland — a review with recommendations. Ulster Trust for Nature Conservation, Belfast.

Clegg, J. (1965) *The Freshwater Life of the British Isles*. Wayside and Woodland Series. 3rd Edition.

Clegg, J. (1969) *The Observer Book of Pond Life*. Fredrick Warne & Co. Ltd., London, England.

Cross, J.R. (1985) The Decline of the Midland Raised Bogs. *The Badger*, Newsletter of the Irish Wildlife Federation, No. 22, pages 10-11.

Cruickshank, J.G. & Wilcock, D.N. (1982) *Northern Ireland Environment and Nature Resources*. The Queen's University of Belfast & The New University of Ulster Publishers, Belfast.

Curtis, T.G.F. & McGough, H.N. (1987). *The Irish Red Data Book: 1 Vascular Plants*. Forest & Wildlife Service, Dublin.

De Buitléar, É. (1984) *Wild Ireland*. Country House, Dublin.

Doyle, G.J. (1983) Conserving Bogland. In *Promise and Performance: Irish Environmental Policies Analysed*. Eds. Blackwell, J. and Convery, F.

Dunlop, D.J. & Christie, S.J. (1987) Peatlands in Northern Ireland. *The Natural World*, Newsletter of the Royal Society for Nature Conservation.

Dunne, J. & Lawlor, P. (1986) *Irish Shooting Companion*. National Association of Regional Game Councils. Elsevier Printers, Shannon.

Glob, P.V. (1977) *The Bog People*. Faber & Faber, London.

Godwin, H. (1981) *The Archives of the Peat Bogs*. Cambridge University Press, London.

Goodhue, D. (1980) *Irish Bogs and Fens*. No. 63 of the Irish Environmental Library Series. Folens, Dublin.

Goodwillie, R. (1980) *European Peatlands*. Nature and Environment Series No. 19, Council of Europe, Strasbourg.

Halpin, A. (1984) *A Preliminary Survey of Archaeological Material Recovered from Peatlands in the Republic of Ireland*. Office of Public Works, Dublin.

Hammond, R.F. (1979) *The Peatlands of Ireland*. Soil Survey Bulletin No. 35. An Foras Talúntais, Dublin.

Herman, D., Geraty, M., O'Hagan, V., Peel, S. & White, B. (1986) *A Plan for Our Hills* A National Park for the Dublin & Wicklow Mountains. Irish Ramblers Club, Dublin.

Hogan, D. (1986) *An Portach — The Bog*. Gasra Stadéir, An Chlocháin agus Muintearas na hOileán, An Togra Oideachais, Gaillimh.

Hywel-Davies, J., Thom, V. & Bennett, L. (1986). *The Macmillan Guide to Britain's Nature Reserves*. Papermac, London & Basingstoke.

Lynch, P. (1983/84) *The Ecology of Bogs*. Bord na Móna, Dublin.

Macan, T.T. (1979) *Freshwater Invertebrate Animals*. Longman, London.

Mellanby, H. (1963) *Animal Life in Freshwater*. 6th Edition. Chapman and Hall, London. Science Reprint (1986).

Mitchell, F. (1986) *The Shell Guide to Reading the Irish Landscape*. Country House, Dublin.

Mitchell, G.F. (1976) *The Irish Landscape*. Collins, London.

Moore, P.D. & Bellamy, D. (1974) *Peatlands*. Elek Science, London.

O'Connell, C.A. (1986) The Future of Irish Raised Bogs. The Resource Source Environment Guide No. 7. Environment Awareness Bureau, Dublin.

O'Rourke, F.J. (1970) *The Fauna of Ireland*. Mercier Press, Cork.

Peterson, R.T., Mountfield, G. & Hollum, P.A.D. (1984) *A Field Guide to the Birds of Britain and Europe*. 4th Edition, Collins, London.

Praeger, R.L. (1934) *The Botanist in Ireland*. Hodges, Figgis & Company, Dublin.

Praeger R.L. (1937) *The Way That I Went*. Allen Figgis Ltd., Dublin.

Quinn, A.C.M. (1984) *Directory of Organisations with Environmental Interests*. An Taisce & National Board for Science & Technology, Dublin.

Reynolds, J. (1984). Vanishing Irish Boglands. *World Wildlife News*, Spring 1984.

Ruttledge, R.F. & Oligvie, M.A. (1979) The past and present status of the Greenland White-fronted Goose in Ireland and Britain. *Irish Birds* 1: 293-363

Ryan, J.B. & Cross, J.R. (1984) Conservation of Peatlands in Ireland. *Proc. of the 7th Int. Peat Congress*, Dublin.

Schouten, M.G.C. (1981) Some Notes on the Preservation of Irish Bogs. Internal Publication, Catholic University, Nijmegen.

Schouten, M.G.C. (1984) Some aspects of the Ecogeographical Gradient in Irish Bogs. *Proc. of the 7th Int. Peat Congress*, Dublin: 388-405

Woods, C.S. (1974) *Freshwater Life in Ireland*. Irish University Press, Dublin.

Van Eck, H., Govers, A., Lemaire, A. & Schaminee, J. (1984) *Irish Bogs A Case for Planning*. Catholic University, Nijmegen.

Webb, D.A. (1977) *An Irish Flora*. Dun Dealgan Press Limited, Dundalk.

Webb, D.A. & Scannell, M.J.P. (1983). *Flora of Connemara and the Burren*. Royal Dublin Society & Cambridge University Press, Cambridge.

APPENDIX 1

Species typical of bogs

Plants of Bogs

Scientific Name	English Name
Andromeda polifolia	Bog Rosemary
Calluna vulgaris	Ling Heather
Carex limosa	Mud Sedge
Carex panicea	Carnation Sedge
Drosera anglica	Great Sundew
Drosera intermedia	Long-leaved Sundew
Drosera rotundifolia	Round-leaved Sundew
Empetrum nigrum	Crowberry
Erica mackaiana	Mackay's Heath
Erica tetralix	Cross-leaved Heath
Eriocaulon aquaticum	Pipewort
Eriophorum angustifolium	Many-flowered Bog Cotton
Eriophorum vaginatum	Bog Cotton
Huperzia selago	Clubmoss
Juniperus communis	Juniper
Lobelia dortmana	Water Lobelia
Menyanthes trifoliata	Bog Bean
Molinia caerulea	Purple Moor Grass
Narthecium ossifragum	Bog Asphodel
Nuphar lutea	Yellow Water-lily
Nymphaea alba	White Water-lily
Pedicularis sylvatica	Lousewort
Pinguicula grandiflora	Great Butterwort
Pinguicula lusitanica	Lusitanian Butterwort
Potentilla erecta	Tormentil
Rhynchospora alba	White Beak Sedge
Rhynchospora fusca	Brown Beak Sedge
Rubus chamaemorus	Cloudberry
Sarracenia purpurea	Pitcher Plant
Schoenus nigricans	Black Bog Rush
Scirpus cespitosus	Deer Sedge
Utricularia minor	Bladderwort
Vaccinium myrtillus	Bilberry
Vaccinium oxycoccus	Cranberry

Mosses & Liverworts of Bogs

Acrocladium cuspidatum
Aneura pinguis
Aulacomnium palustre
Calypogeia fissa
Calypogeia muellerana
Calypogeia sphagnicola
Campylopus atrovirens

Campylopus introflexus
Campylopus paradoxus
Cladopodiella fluitans
Cephalozia bicuspidata
Cephalozia connivens
Dicranum scoparium
Diplophyllum albicans
Eurhynchium praelongum
Frullania dilatata
Frullania tamarisci
Hylocomnium splendens   Red Feather Moss
Hypnum jutlandicum
Kurzia pauciflora
Leucobryum glaucum   Cushion Moss
Lophocolea cuspidata
Lophozia ventricosa
Mylia anomala
Mylia taylori
Odontoschisma sphagni
Plagiothecium undulatum
Pleurozia purpurea
Pleurozium schreberi
Polytrichum alpestre
Polytrichum commune
Pohlia nutans
Pseudoscleropodium purum
Racomitrium lanuginosum   Silver-haired Moss
Rhytidiadelphus loreus
Sphagnum auriculatum   Bog Moss
Sphagnum capillifolium   Bog Moss
Sphagnum compactum   Bog Moss
Sphagnum cuspidatum   Aquatic Bog Moss
Sphagnum fuscum   Bog Moss
Sphagnum imbricatum   Bog Moss
Sphagnum magellanicum   Bog Moss
Sphagnum palustre   Bog Moss
Sphagnum papillosum   Bog Moss
Sphagnum pulchrum   Aquatic Bog Moss
Sphagnum recurvum   Bog Moss
Sphagnum subnitens   Bog Moss
Sphagnum subsecundum   Aquatic Bog Moss
Sphagnum tenellum   Bog Moss
Thuidium tamariscinum

Algae of Bogs

Zygogonium ericetorum

Lichens of Bogs

Cladonia arbuscula
Cladonia bellidiflora

Cladonia crispata	
Cladonia fimbriata	Slender Cladonia
Cladonia floerkeana	Matchstick Lichen
Cladonia furcata	
Cladonia portentosa	Branching Cladonia
Cladonia pyxidata	Cup Lichen
Cladonia rangiferina	Reindeer Lichen
Cladonia tenuis	
Cladonia uncialis	
Cladonia verticillata	
Cornicularia aculeata	
Evernia prunastri	Oak Moss
Hypogymnia physodes	
Hypogymnia tubulosa	
Peltigera canina	Dog Lichen
Peltigera polydactyla	
Pertusaria amara	
Parmelia caperata	Crottle
Parmelia glabratula	Crottle
Parmelia sulcata	Crottle
Physcia tenella	
Ramalina farinacea	
Ramalina fastigiata	
Ramalina fraxinea	
Usnea subloridana	Beard Lichen
Xanthoria parietina	Yellow Scales Lichen

APPENDIX 2

Species typical of internal drainage systems on bogs

Plants of Soak Systems on Raised Bogs

Scientific Name	English Name
Agrostis canina	Bent Grass
Agrostis stolonifera	Bent Grass
Angelica sylvestris	Angelica
Anthoxanthum odoratum	Sweet Vernal Grass
Betula pubescens	Birch
Carex curta	White Sedge
Carex echinata	Star Sedge
Carex nigra	Black Sedge
Carex rostrata	Bottle Sedge
Dactylorhiza maculata	Spotted Orchid
Dryopteris carthusiana	Narrow Buckler-fern
Dryopteris dilatata	Broad Buckler-fern
Empetrum nigrum	Crowberry
Epilobium obscurum	Willow Herb
Festuca rubra	Red Fescue
Galium palustre	Water Bedstraw
Galium saxatile	Heath Bedstraw
Hedera helix	Ivy
Holcus lanatus	Yorkshire Fog
Hydrocotyle vulgaris	Marsh Pennywort
Juncus effusus	Soft Rush
Luzula multiflora	Many-headed Wood-rush
Lychnis flos-cuculi	Ragged Robin
Menyanthes trifoliata	Bog Bean
Molinia caerulea	Purple Moor Grass
Myrica gale	Bog Myrtle
Osmunda regalis	Royal Fern
Potentilla erecta	Tormentil
Potentill palustris	Marsh Cinquefoil
Rubus fruticosus agg.	Bramble
Rumex acetosa	Sorrel
Succisa pratensis	Devil's Bit Scabious
Typha latifolia	Bulrush
Vaccinium myrtillus	Bilberry
Vaccinium oxycoccus	Cranberry

Mosses & Liverworts of Soak Systems on Raised Bogs

Aulacomnium palustre
Calliergon cuspidatum
Calypogeia fissa
Calypogeia muellerana
Drepanocladus revolvens

Eurhynchium praelongum	
Hylocomium brevirostre	
Hylocomnium splendens	Red Feather Moss
Hypnum jutlandicum	
Lophocolea cuspidata	
Mnium hornum	
Odontoschisma sphagni	
Pleurozium schreberi	
Polytrichum alpestre	
Polytrichum commune	
Pseudoscleropodium purum	
Rhytidiadelphus squarrosus	
Rytidiadelphus triquetrus	
Sphagnum capillifolium	Bog Moss
Sphagnum cuspidatum	Aquatic Bog Moss
Sphagnum fimbriatum	Bog Moss
Sphagnum magellanicum	Bog Moss
Sphagnum palustre	Bog Moss
Sphagnum papillosum	Bog Moss
Sphagnum recurvum	Bog Moss
Sphagnum squarrosum	Bog Moss
Sphagnum subnitens	Bog Moss
Thuidium tamariscinum	
Ulota crispa	

Lichens of Soak Systems of Raised Bogs

Cladonia portentosa	
Desmococcus viridis	
Evernia prunastri	Oak Moss
Hypogymnia physodes	
Parmelia caperata	Crottle
Parmelia glabratula	Crottle
Parmelia sulcata	Crottle
Ramalina farinacea	
Ramalina fastigiata	
Usnea subflorida	Beard Lichen

Plants of Swallow Holes on Blanket Bogs

Agrostis stolonifera	Bent Grass
Anthoxanthum odoratum	Sweet Vernal Grass
Athyrium filix-femina	Lady Fern
Blechnum spicant	Hard Fern
Calluna vulgaris	Ling Heather
Carex echinata	Star Sedge
Carex flacca	Glaucous Sedge
Carex nigra	Black Sedge
Dactylorhiza maculata	Spotted Orchid
Dryopteris aemula	Hay-scented Buckler-fern

Dryopteris carthusiana	Narrow Buckler-fern
Dryopteris dilatata	Broad Buckler-fern
Erica cinerea	Bell Heather
Galium palustre	Water Bedstraw
Galium saxatile	Heath Bedstraw
Holcus lanatus	Yorkshire Fog
Juncus bulbosus	Bulbous Rush
Juncus effusus	Common Rush
Luzula multiflora	Many-headed Wood-rush
Lonicera periclymenum	Honeysuckle
Osmunda regalis	Royal Fern
Potentilla erecta	Tormentil
Ranunculus flammula	Lesser Spearwort
Rubus fruticosus	Brambles
Rumex acetosa	Sorrel
Succisa pratensis	Devil's Bit Scabious

Mosses & Liverworts of Swallow Holes on Blanket Bogs

Eurhynchium praelongum	
Hylocomium splendens	Red Feather Moss
Hypnum cupressiforme	
Mnium hornum	
Plagiothecium undulatum	
Pleurozium schreberi	
Polytrichum commune	Common Hair Moss
Sphagnum palustre	Bog Moss

Plants of Surface Drains on Blanket Bogs

Anthoxanthum odoratum	Sweet Vernal Grass
Agrostis stolonifera	Bent Grass
Cardamine pratensis	Lady's Smock
Carex demissa	Common Yellow Sedge
Carex limosa	Mud Sedge
Carex nigra	Black Sedge
Carex panicea	Carnation Sedge
Carex paniculata	Greater Tussock Sedge
Carex rostrata	Bottle Sedge
Eleocharis multicaulis	Many-stemmed Spike-rush
Equisetum fluviatile	Water Horsetail
Erica tetralix	Cross-leaved Heath
Eriophorum angustifolium	Many-flowered Bog Cotton
Eriophorum vaginatum	Bog Cotton
Galium palustre	Water Bedstraw
Hippuris vulgaris	Mare's Tail
Holcus lanatus	Yorkshire Fog
Hydrocotyle vulgaris	Marsh Pennywort
Juncus articulatus	Jointed Rush

Juncus bulbosus	Bulbous Rush
Juncus effusus	Soft Rush
Malaxis paludosa	Bog Orchid
Mentha aquatica	Mint
Menyanthes trifoliata	Bog Bean
Molinia caerulea	Purple Moor Grass
Myrica gale	Bog Myrtle
Narthecium ossifragum	Bog Asphodel
Pedicularis palustris	Red Rattle
Potamogeton coloratus	Pondweed
Potentilla erecta	Tormentil
Potentilla palustris	Marsh Cinquefoil
Ranunculus flammula	Lesser Spearwort
Rhynchospora alba	White Beak Sedge
Rubus fruticosus	Bramble
Rumex acetosa	Sorrel
Salix atrocinerea	Willow
Salix aurita	Willow
Schoenus nigricans	Black Bog Rush
Veronica beccabunga	Brooklime

Mosses of Surface Drains on Blanket Bogs

Aulacomnium palustre	
Hypnum cupressiforme	
Pleurozium schreberi	
Rhytidiadelphus loreus	
Sphagnum auriculatum	Bog Moss
Sphagnum capillifolium	Bog Moss
Sphagnum cuspidatum	Aquatic Bog Moss
Sphagnum palustre	Bog Moss
Sphagnum recurvum	Bog Moss

APPENDIX 3

Species typical of fens

Plants of Fens	
Scientific Name	English Name
Agrostis stolonifera	Bent Grass
Alnus glutinosa	Alder
Angelica sylvestris	Angelica
Anthoxanthum odoratum	Sweet Vernal Grass
Betula pubescens	Birch
Briza media	Quaking Grass
Calluna vulgaris	Ling Heather
Caltha palustris	Marsh Marigold, Kingcup
Cardamine pratensis	Lady's Smock
Carex appropinguata	Fibrous Tussock Sedge
Carex demissa	Common Yellow Sedge
Carex disticha	Brown Sedge
Carex flacca	Glaucous Sedge
Carex lasiocarpa	Slender Sedge
Carex lepidocarpa	Fen Sedge
Carex limosa	Mud Sedge
Carex nigra	Black Sedge
Carex panicea	Carnation Sedge
Carex pulicaris	Flea Sedge
Carex rostrata	Bottle Sedge
Centaurea nigra	Blackheads
Chara sp.	Stonewort
Cirsium dissectum	Fen Thistle
Cladium mariscus	Saw Sedge
Dactylorhiza incarnata	Marsh Orchid
Dactylorhiza traunsteineri	Orchid
Drosera rotundifolia	Round-leaved Sundew
Equisetum fluviatile	Water Horsetail
Erica tetralix	Cross-leaved Heath
Eriophorum gracile	Bog Cotton
Eriophorum latifolium	Fen Bog Cotton
Eupatorium cannabinum	Hemp Agrimony
Festuca rubra	Red Fescue
Filipendula ulmaria	Meadowsweet
Galium uliginosum	Marsh Bedstraw
Geranium robertianum	Herb Robert
Glyceria fluitans	Float Grass
Gymnadenia conopsea	Fragrant Orchid
Holcus lanatus	Yorkshire Fog
Hydrocharis morsus-ranae	Frog-bit
Hydrocotyle vulgaris	Marsh Pennywort
Hypericum pulchrum	Slender St. John's Wort
Juncus acutiflorus	Sharp-flowered Rush
Juncus articulatus	Jointed Rush
Juncus subnodulosus	Blunt-flowered Rush
Lathyrus palustris	Marsh Pea

Lathyrus pratensis	Meadow Vetchling
Lemna minor	Duckweed
Luzula multiflora	Many-headed Wood-rush
Lychnis flos-cuculi	Ragged Robin
Malaxis paludosa	Bog Orchid
Mentha aquatica	Mint
Menyanthes trifoliata	Bog Bean
Molinia caerulea	Purple Moor Grass
Narthecium ossifragum	Bog Asphodel
Nasturtium officinale	Water Cress
Ophrys insectifera	Fly Orchid
Parnassia palustris	Grass of Parnassus
Pedicularis sylvatica	Red Rattle
Phragmites australis	Common Reed
Pinguicula vulgaris	Butterwort
Potamogeton coloratus	Pondweed
Potentilla palustris	Marsh Cinquefoil
Pyrola rotundifolia	Wintergreen
Ranunculus flammula	Lesser Spearwort
Salix aurita	Willow
Schoenus nigricans	Black Bog Rush
Sparganium erectum	Bur-reed
Succisa pratensis	Devil's Bit Scabious
Thelypteris palustris	Marsh Fern
Trifolium repens	White Clover
Triglochin palustris	Arrow Grass
Utricularia intermedia	Bladderwort
Utricularia vulgaris	Bladderwort
Vaccinium oxycoccus	Cranberry
Valeriana officinalis	Wild Valerian
Veronica beccabunga	Brooklime

Mosses & Liverworts of Fens

Aulacomnium palustre	
Brachythecium rutabulum	
Bryum pseudotriquetrum	
Ctenidium molluscum	
Calliergon cuspidatum	Spear Moss
Calliergon giganteum	
Camptothecium nitens	
Campylium stellatum	
Cinclidium stygium	
Climacium dendroides	
Drepanocladus fluitans	
Drepanocladus revolvens	
Hylocomnium splendens	Red Feather Moss
Mnium hornum	
Mnium undulatum	
Pseudoscleropodium purum	
Rhytidiadelphus squarrosus	
Riccardia pinguis	
Scorpidium scorpioides	
Sphagnum palustre	Bog Moss
Sphagnum squarrosum	Bog Moss
Sphagnum subnitens	Bog Moss

APPENDIX 4

Selected animals occurring on bogs and fens

Class/Order/Species Scientific Name	English Name

Habitat B = bog, F = fen

Gastropoda Vertiginidae (Land Snails)
Arion ater — Large Black Slug B,F
Vertigo geyeri — Snail F

Pisces (Fish)
Gasterosteus aculeatus — Three-spined Stickleback F
Pungilius pungilius — Ten-spined Stickleback F

Amphibia (Amphibians)
Rana temporaria — Common Frog B,F
Triturus vulgaris — Common Newt F

Reptilia (Reptiles)
Lacerta vivipara — Viviparous or Common Lizard B

Aves (Birds)
R = Resident   Sv = Summer visitor   Wv = Winter visitor   Ov = Occasional visitor

Accipiter nisus — Sparrowhawk Ov F
Acrocephalus schoenobaenus — Sedge Warbler Sv F
Alauda arvensis — Skylark R B,F
Anas acuta — Pintail Wv F
Anas clypeata — Shoveler Wv F
Anas crecca — Teal Wv,Sv B,F
Anas penelope — Wigeon Wv F
Anas platyrhynchos — Mallard R,Wv B,F
Anas strepera — Gadwall Ov F
Anser albifrons flavirostris — Greenland White-fronted Goose Wv B
Anthus pratensis — Meadow Pipit R B,F
Ardea cinerea — Grey Heron Ov B,F
Aythya ferina — Pochard Wv F
Aythya fuligula — Tufted Duck Wv F
Carduelis cannabina — Linnet Sv, Wv B,F
Carduelis carduelis — Goldfinch Ov F
Carduelis chloris — Greenfinch R, Wv F
Carduelis flammea — Redpoll Ov F
Circus cyaneus — Hen Harrier Ov,Sv B,F
Corvus corax — Raven R B
Corvus corone cornix — Hooded Crow R B
Cuculus canorus — Cuckoo Sv B,F
Cygnus cygnus — Whooper Swan Wv F
Cygnus olor — Mute Swan R F
Delichon urbica — House Martin Sv F
Emberiza schoeniclus — Reed Bunting R F
Erithacus rubecula — Robin R F
Falco columbarius — Merlin Sv,Ov B,F

Falco peregrinus	Peregrine Sv,Ov B,F
Falco tinnunculus	Kestrel Sv,Ov B,F
Fringilla coelebs	Chaffinch Wv F
Fringilla montifringilla	Brambling Ov F
Fulica atra	Coot R F
Gallinago gallinago	Snipe R,Wv B,F
Gallinula chloropus	Moorhen R F
Hirundo rustica	Swallow Sv B,F
Lagopus lagopus	Red Grouse R B
Larus ridibundus	Black-headed Gull Sv F
Locustella naevia	Grasshopper Warbler Sv F
Lymnocryptes minimus	Jack Snipe Wv B,F
Muscicapa striata	Spotted Flycatcher Sv F
Numenius arquata	Curlew Wv,Sv B,F
Oenanthe oenanthe	Wheatear Sv B,F
Phylloscopus collybita	Chiffchaff Sv F
Phylloscopus trochilus	Willow Warbler Sv F
Pluvialis apricaria	Golden Plover Wv,Sv B,F
Podiceps cristatus	Great Crested Grebe R,Wv F
Prunella modularis	Dunnock R F
Rallus aquaticus	Water Rail R F
Riparia riparia	Sand Martin Sv F
Saxicola rubetra	Whinchat Sv B,F
Saxicola torquata	Stonechat R B,F
Sylvia communis	Whitethroat Sv F
Tachybaptus ruficollis	Little Grebe R F
Tringa totanus	Redshank Wv F
Troglodytes troglodytes	Wren R F
Turdus merula	Blackbird R F
Turdus philomelos	Song Thrush R F
Vanellus vanellus	Lapwing R,Wv F

Mammalia (Mammals)

Capra	Feral Goat B
Cervus elaphus	Red Deer B
Lepus timidus	Irish Hare B
Lutra lutra	Otter F
Mustela vison	American Mink F
Oryctolagus cuniculus	Rabbit B,F
Sorex minutus	Pygmy Shrew B,F
Vulpes vulpes	Fox B,F

APPENDIX 5

Selected taxa of invertebrates which occur on bogs and fens and examples of families or species.

Class/Order/Family/Species Scientific Name	English Name

Status W = widely distributed, L = local and V = vulnerable

Habitat B = bog, F = fen, FC = fen carr, * = frequent in other habitats besides peatlands, BP = bog pools and WB = bog woodlands (for example those associated with soak systems)

Crustacea Cladocera (Water Fleas)
Macrothricidae
Chydoridae

Amphipoda
Gammarus duebeni   Freshwater Shrimp W F*

Arachnida Araneae (Spiders)
Arygrometa aquatica   Water Spider W BP
Dolomedes fimbriatus   Bog-pool Spider L BP

Acari (Mites)
Hydracarina   Water Mite

Insecta Collembola (Spring-tails)
Poduridae
Isotomidae

Ephemeroptera (Mayflies)

Odonta (Dragonflies & Damselflies)
Brachytron pratense   Hairy Dragonfly L F*
Coenagrion puella   Azure Damselfly W B,F*
Enallagma cyathigerum   Common Blue Damselfly W B,F*
Ischnura elegans   Common IschnuraW B,F*
Lestes sponsa   Emerald Damselfly L B,F
Libellula quadrimaculata   Four-spotted Chaser W B,F*
Pyrrhosoma nymphula   Large Red Damselfly W B,F*
Sympetrum scoticum   Black Darter W B
Sympetrum striolatum   Common Sympetrum W B,F*

Orthoptera (Grasshoppers and Crickets)
Omocestus viridis   Green Grasshopper W B,F*
Tetrix subulata   Fen Ground Hopper W F
Tetrix undulata   Bog Ground Hopper W B
Stethophyma grossa   Great Green Bog Grasshopper V B

Hemiptera (True Bugs)
Aphrophora alni   Frog Bug W B,F
Corixa species   Water Bugs W B,P*
Gigara species   Water Bugs W B,P*
Neophilaenus lineatus   Moorland Cuckoo-spit Bug W B,F
Notonecta glauca   Water Boatman W B,P*

Gerridae (Pond Skaters)

Veliidae (Water Crickets)

Acanthosomidae (Shieldbugs)

Lepidoptera (Moths & Butterflies)

Aglais urticae	Small Tortoiseshell W B,F*
Aphantopus hyperantus	Ringlet W B,F*
Callophrys rubi	Green Hairstreak L B,F*
Coenonympha pamphilus	Small Heath W B,F*
Coenonympha tullia	Large Heath L B
Euphydryas aurinia	Marsh Fritillary L F
Gonepteryx rhamni	Brimstone L F*
Lasiocampa quercus	Oak Eggar W B,F*
Leptidea sinapis	Wood White L F*
Lycaena phlaeas	Small Copper W B,F*
Macrothylacia rubi	Fox Moth W B,F*
Maniola jurtina	Meadow Brown W B,F*
Noctua pronuba	Large Yellow Underwing B
Nymphalis io	Peacock W B,F*
Pararge aegeria	Speckled Wood W B,F*
Parasemia plantaginis	Wood Tiger L B
Polyommatus icarus	Common Blue W B,F*
Saturnia pavonia	Emperor Moth W B,F*
Smerinthus ocellata	Eyed Hawk W F,C*
Spilosoma lutea	Buff Ermine B

Trichoptera (Caddis Flies)
Limnephilidae
Polycentropidae

Diptera (True Flies)

Herina fiondescentiae	Fen Picture-wing Fly W F*
Lipara lucens	Cigar Gall Fly L F*
Tachina grossa	Fox-moth Parasite Fly L B,F*

Ephydridae (Marsh-flies)

W B,F*

Tabanidae (Horse-flies)

Chrysops sepulchralis	Small Horse-fly L F
Haematopota pluvialis	Cleg W B,F*
Hybomitra montana	Bog Horse Fly L B
Hybomitra muhlfeldi	Bog Woodland Horse Fly V W,B

Syrphidae (Hover-flies)

Anasimyia lineata	W B,F
Chrysagastra hirtella	W B,F*
Eristalis species	W B,F*
Helophilus hybridus	L F*
Lejogaster metallina	W B,F*
Neoascia tenur	W B,F*
Sericomyia silentis	W B,F*
Syritta pipiens	W B,F*
Volucella bombylans	W B,F*

Tipulidae (Craneflies)
Dictaenidia bimaculata   Large Cranefly V WB

Rhagionidae (Snipe-flies)
Chrysopilus auratus   Golden Snipe Fly W B,F*
Rhagio scolopacea   Spotted Snipe Fly W F,C*

Dolichopodidae (Long-headed Flies)   W B,F*

Chironomidae (Non-biting midges)   W B,F*

Ceratopogonidae (Biting midges)   W B,F*

Hymenoptera (Bees, Wasps, Ants, Sawflies)
Bombus lucorum   Bumble Bee W B,F*
Bombus muscorum   Ginger Bog Bumble Bee W B,F*
Cimbex femorata   Birch Sawfly L B,F*
Dolerus cothurnatus   Red-banded Sawfly W B,F
Dolerus species   Red-banded Sawflies W B,F
Myrmica ruginodis   Red Ant W B,F*
Tenthredo moniliata   Bog Bean Sawfly L B
Vespula rufa   Red Wasp W B,F

Coleoptera (Beetles)
Aromia moschata   Musk Beetle V FC
Carabus granulatus   Green Fen Ground Beetle W B,F*
Donacia species   Leaf Beetle W B,F
Lochmaea suturalis   Heather Beetle W B*
Plateumaris species   Leaf Beetle W B,F*
Plateumaris discolor   Leaf Beetle W B,F*
Phyllodecta suturalis   Sallow Leaf Beetle W F,C*

Silphidae (Burying Beetles)

Staphylinidae (Rove Beetles)

Dytiscidae (Water Beetles)
Agabus arcticus   Northern Water Beetle L BP

APPENDIX 6

Tables for use in the student investigations

Table 1: Calculation of soil moisture content.

$$\% \text{ moisture content } = \frac{\text{weight loss in oven}}{\text{wet soil weight}} \times 100$$

Site	Tin No.	Tin wt.	Tin + wet soil	Wet soil wt.	Tin + dry soil	Dry soil wt.	Loss in wt.	% moisture

Table 2: Calculation of soil organic content.

$$\% \text{ organic content } = \frac{\text{weight loss on burning}}{\text{dry soil weight}} \times 100$$

Site	Tin + burnt soil	Burnt soil weight	Weight loss on burning (dry weight − burnt weight)	% Organic

Table 3: Vegetation analysis field data sheet.

SAMPLING SITE..............................

DATE..............................

SPECIES	QUADRAT NUMBER										TOTAL OCCURRENCE
	1	2	3	4	5	6	7	8	9	10	
SITE DATA											AVERAGE
Soil Depth (cm)											
pH											
% Moisture											
% Organic											

Table 4: Vegetation data, a summary of the % frequency of species in two different habitats.

Calculation of the % frequency.

$$\% \text{ Frequency} = \frac{\text{number of quadrats where the species is present}}{\text{total number of quadrats}} \times 100$$

SIZE OF QUADRAT: NO. OF QUADRATS PER SITE:

SPECIES	% FREQUENCY	
	BOG PROPER	CUTAWAY BOG

INDEX